Truth Beyond the Earthly Matrix

Truth Beyond the Earthly Matrix

UNDERSTANDING THE EARTHLY PROGRAMS OF LIMITATIONS AND CONTROLS

Ronald R Fellion DD

ISBN: 0997096403
Paper back ISBN 9780997096408

E-Book ISBN 978-0-9970964-1-5

A special thanks to Krysta Bell for reading through this book and her suggestions for helping to ensure the information is understandable.

This book is dedicated to those who feel there is more beyond this world-reality. It's to those who have a desire to seek and understand the truths that have been hidden from them rather than simply believe what they have been taught-told on this world.

"When an individual and/or a society get to the point where they automatically accept the ideas and concepts we are taught without question, we have stopped growing-learning. It is only by questioning the accepted that we can expand and grow beyond what we knew."

Ronald Fellion

Table of contents

Introduction

"PHYSICALITY DOES NOT EXIST! REALITY does not exist! All that exist is nothing!"

Take a moment to read the above statement again and if it's true, think about how it would effect-impact your life.

All the information contained in this book is based on the above statement being true and how it impacts all the thoughts and beliefs-truths we have accepted.   Keep the above statement in mind as you read this book and it may help your understanding of the ideas and concepts presented.

How do you put a feeling-knowing-understanding in to words when those words don't exist because the concepts are beyond our verbal language? Many places in this book you will see that I put words together to express a concept or feeling because it's as close as I can come using the English language. I am not saying this as an excuse but to explain why the book is written as it is.

As you are reading these ideas and concepts you may get a knowing-understanding-feeling beyond what is written on the pages and that is my goal in writing it as I did.

Most of the concepts in this book are not accepted main stream metaphysical-new age beliefs.

When I say accepted metaphysical beliefs I am referring to those concepts and theories that people accept because someone said that's the way it is and always has been.

An example of an accepted belief is that we have to ascend to higher dimensions to obtain enlightenment, and we have to work our way through many levels to accomplish this. A lot of what spiritual people are told they have to do is based on this belief.

After receiving-remembering information I no longer accept the need for ascension as being true and will explain why in chapter 11.

My goal in writing this book is to get people to open their minds and look at what they have learned in a different way rather than accepting what others say-write as truth just because it's what others have always believed.

This book contains the information I have remembered-received over the last few years and is also based on the many experiences I have had in dreams, energy sessions with others, and journeys outside my body, all of which showed me how this information applies in and beyond this reality.

I believe it's only by questioning-examining what you hear and read from others that you will get to and understand the truth. If what you see and hear feels right inside as something that is true, pay attention and see where that information will lead you. Don't accept what you see or hear as a final truth and stop searching, because that truth is only one branch on the tree of your journey.

If the information doesn't feel right don't accept it as a truth just because it was written or said by someone who is well known, has a following, or because this information is accepted by others.

There is some truth in everything and it is your job to seek-pick it out. It's only by questioning and examining what you hear and read that you will be able to find the gold hidden within the sand.

I am presenting these ideas and concepts based on my experiences-knowing. If they feel right or resonate inside you as being true, take them and see where that information leads you on your journey to find the truth. This book doesn't have all the answers but it may show you-open a path that leads to new answers-truths.

You may find that some information changes throughout the book as I followed my path to-search for the truth, but I wanted to leave all the information in because it may be helpful to some.

We may walk together on this journey for a time, but at some point everyone will have to walk their own path if they are truly seeking the truth. Others can tell you about their journey and experiences and that may give you a jump start on your journey, but if they are telling you that their path is the only one that leads to the truth, you should turn around and run the other way. The odds are their path to the truth has a price tag and they are making a nice living selling it.

I believe the truth is owned by all and should be shared as freely as possible with all who want to learn.

Thank you for taking the time to read this book and sharing with others any truths you have gained.

The more people that open their mind to possibilities, the more spirits we can free from this dream.

I didn't write this book to make you think like I do, I wrote it to make you think.

If you have questions or feedback feel free to contact me on our face book page at, "Temple of Universal Truth," or email me at **tutruth1213@ gmail.com**.

We have a website that is currently a work in progress and will post on facebook when it is done.

In the meantime enjoy your search for truth after all it's why we are here.

CHAPTER 1

Defining Words such as God, Source, Ego Mind, consciousness and Others.

I WOULD LIKE TO DEFINE some of the words I will be using in this book because each of these words means different things to different people and I want to make sure you understand the meaning of how I am using them. Your definition may be different and that is ok.

Real: In order for something to be real it must always exist. Anything that is created has a beginning and an end and anything that ends can't be real.

God: Most people use this word to identify a being that is outside of, separate from, and greater than they are. I believe we are one, it is us and we are it, there is no separation and no one to worship or try to please.

Spirit Guides: Aspects of us-we are aspects of them. It's an aspect of us that stayed outside the physical realm in order to see the big picture. They help and guide us and are aware of all realities, possibilities, and paths.

Nothing: This is all that is real. It created-became source when it had a thought to experience itself on all levels and possibilities at once.

Source-Unconscious mind: This is what everything is, we are a part of it and it is all of us.

Source created all that is in a single thought and we are part of that thought. It is not beyond or separate from us.

Universe: A universe is our reality not what science calls outer space and what we can see in the night sky.

Religion: Any time you have to follow defined steps-procedures-rules in order to reach a goal and others are required to do the same. Any time there are rules that say if you don't follow their path you will not be able to reach the goal on your own, that their path-route is the only one that is correct. This can be following a person, a club, group, or organization. It's a part of any belief that someone or thing outside of you is required to help you gain another level or place.

Brain: The computer of our physical form. It creates whatever happens within the physical body based on the programming it receives from the ego mind. The brain doesn't care or have awareness of what it's doing to our physical body. It's only following what it's programmed to do.

Ego mind: It's the default loading program for the brain and all information we receive from our 5 senses on this world. The ego mind exists within this false universe on all levels and in all beings that have a physical structure.

Consciousness: The connection between the spirit world and the physical world. It is the connection between our subconscious (spirit) and ego mind (physical) allowing us to receive-remember information from outside the physical realm and program it in to the brain. It isn't needed unless we are in physical form.

Subconscious: This is us outside the physical realm but within this universe. This presence is known as our spirit guide/s and is directly connected to source-our unconscious mind. When we go with our intuition, inner self, higher self we are connecting with our subconscious mind. All information from the subconscious mine passes through the conscious mind to the ego mind and is imputed in to the brain. This aspect of us sees all time lines or paths within this universe and is connected to all aspects of us within this universe.

Creation: Anything that has a beginning and thus an end is a creation and creations aren't real because they are temporary.

Awareness: This what most people refer to as consciousness but I believe awareness and consciousness are different. As I said above consciousness is the connection between the physical and spirit, and awareness indicates a knowing you exist separate from that around you.

Time: A creation that has a beginning and an end no matter how long or short.

Eternal: This word means something that is forever which means it would have to have always been and always will be.

Idea: An idea is a thought that has started to grow and develop. The idea of getting back what you put out is an idea, karma is the concept.

Concept: An idea that has been developed to the point where it has become accepted.

Belief: A concept that has become accepted as a truth. That you need a savior in order to leave this world and go to a better place is a belief, usually no evidence to support it. An example would be reading the bible about heaven existing and believing it without having seen it.

Knowing: Beyond a belief, the person had an experience which shows them, gives them proof the concept is real. They live what they know. Heart knowledge not head knowledge.

Words, their meanings are important.

I heard someone during an interview referring to spirit beings that exists both outside and within our physical reality and they said you can call them spirit guides or angels, or any term you want. They said that the terms or words we use don't matter.

In the past I have used the same concept when talking with others in reference to spiritual beings in order to establish a common point of reference. I have since come to understand this is wrong. Words and the terms we use does matter.

Each word we use to describe spirit beings whether it's god, source, creator, spirit guides, or angels has an accepted meaning. These names-words have creative power and each time we use them it helps the beings we are referring to continue to exist.

A house that isn't lived in will break down very quickly whereas a house that is lived in and taken care of will last a long time. This is because of the energy a house is given by the people living there and the lack of energy given to a house where no one lives. The same is true of the beings we have created and given names to.

Each of these words also comes with a definition within each of our minds and when one person is saying spirit guides and another is saying angels, how they see these beings and their roles, is very different. All spirit beings are not the same anymore than all bees are helpful.

Yes they are all made from the same energy, but their roles and how they interact with us is different.

Let me give you an example. When most people use the term god they are usually referring to a being outside of, better than, and beyond themselves. A being that created humans and is someone whose rules we have to follow to be accepted. We need them to leave this world and go to a better place.

When metaphysical people use the term source they are referring to that from which we all came, it is us and we are it. It isn't better than or outside of us but we are one in the same.

Look closely at the definitions of these two words and you will quickly see we are talking about completely different beings with completely different roles.

A metaphysical person talking to a religious person, who uses the term source and then tells the religious person they can use the term god because the name you use isn't important, is wrong because they are talking about completely different concepts-beings in their minds. One being you're one with, the other you are a slave-servant of. One you can always return to, are always a part of (source) and the other you have to work on returning to and will always be in fear that you wouldn't make it.

When people hear the word angels they think of beings created by and working for god. Yes this includes all angels including Satan and his fallen angels.

Remember they were all supposedly created by god and since everything that happens is part of gods' plan and nothing can happen against his will, it means Satan and his fallen angels are stilling only doing what is part of gods' plan and according to his will. So all angels work for god and can't do anything for us unless it's part of gods' plan or according to his will. In other words they don't have our best interest at heart.

My knowing is that spirit guides are aspects of us-are us that stayed within the spiritual realm in order to guide us since we have forgotten what we are. They have our best interest at heart because they are us and are only working for-with us.

You can see the meanings for angels and spirit guides refer to different beings with completely different roles in how they interact with us.

I am not saying you can't use these terms interchangeable if you and the other person are on the same page.

My suggestion would be that you ask them how they define the term/s they are using and then give them your definition.

You both may have the same definition for spirit guides and angels, source and god, but you should find that out before you start interchanging terms because everything you discuss will be filtered by how each of you define the words you are using.

CHAPTER 2

Sin and Karma, Matrix Traps for Fear and Guilt

SIN AND KARMA ARE TWO concepts-beliefs that rule the religious world in one form or another and are known of and/or understood by pretty much everyone on this planet, but are they real? Do they exist beyond this dream world and why were these concepts put in place?

THE CONCEPT OF KARMA

What does sin and karma mean to people on earth? Karma is the idea that how you live your life determines whether you will get rewards or punishment in this life and the next. If you do well you will get good back and if you do bad things you get bad things back. Kind of like stacking up markers and someone is keeping score on a chalk board to see if you balance out. It's only when you finally balance out that you can move on to another world-level.

One of the problems with Karma is its thought of-known as a karmic circle like the saying what comes around goes around. The phrases karmic circle, circle of life, and what comes around goes around are phrases that most everyone has heard of.

These sayings-ideas have become accepted as truth or possible truths and are part of the default programming on this world.

Because these sayings have been accepted and repeated many times they influence the way people think, view life on this world, and the afterlife. It's been programmed in to the brain as a possibility or belief which affects every area of our lives. It also affects the number of times we incarnate and how long we are trapped in this dream world.

Remember from chapter one the words we use to describe things have meaning and the term karmic circle is no different. Every word used by religions and developed for this world was done to keep the default programming in place and enforces it through the accepted meanings in-of words.

Let's look at the word circle and how something becomes defined as a circle. A circle is a line where any point on the line is an equal distance from the center and the circle line is unbroken. If the line is unbroken which it has to be in order to be a circle, it means you have no way of getting out without breaking the circle.

If what you do or have done in your past life leads to what happens to you tomorrow and what you do in this life leads to what happens to you in the next life, there is no way to break the circle because the past determines the future and you can't change the past.

This means if you believe you are stuck in a karmic circle you will always be stuck and unable to ever leave this-that dream reality.

The idea of being good enough in one life to allow you to escape the circle is a false hope promised to be delivered to its believers only after they die. This is just like the concept that you are always a sinner until after you die.

It's amazing how quickly and how many people buy in to the idea of giving now and getting rewarded only after they die. It's the ego that wants to live on and accepts whatever hope it is given to accomplish that goal. Isn't it interesting that people believe the idea of getting rewarded after death, yet when they see a sign that says wet paint they have to touch to see if it's true?

I often ask people if they ceased to exist after death would they know it. Since the answer has to be no they wouldn't know if they didn't exist after death otherwise they would be still be existing, I then ask why you would worry about something you wouldn't even know happened.

When we think in terms of our lives-experiences here being a circle we are trapping ourselves within this circle, meaning we can never grow beyond it.

We can only move forward along the circle for so long until we are back at our starting point and have to repeat the same path we just completed, meaning we are going backwards rather than forward in our growth. It's like driving round and round in a roundabout and wondering why you never get where you want to go.

People think because they keep getting the same lessons over and over in their lives (meaning they think they haven't learned it yet), that they are trapped within this karmic circle. This way of thinking-believing will ensure they keep having those types of experiences over and over. It's only when you really look at the experiences individually that you will see that they are never actually the same, even though they appear so on the surface.

Rather than thinking of your life as a circle, karmic or otherwise thus trapping yourself, think of your life as a spiral. A spiral goes from a starting point and wraps around its center always moving outward, and more importantly forward.

The spirals can be very close together which will allow incidents to be similar, yet not identical because they are on another wrap of the spiral.

As you experience those lessons and gain greater growth, the spirals can become farther apart allowing the lessons-experiences to be very different.

If you want to change your life, change how you think. Rather than thinking in terms of living in a circle and trapping yourself, think in terms of living in a spiral and you will always be moving forward with no end to the amount of spirals and experiences you can have, and you can get off-out at any time.

THE CONCEPT OF SIN

The concept of sin claims everyone is born in to sin because of the first humans and that as long as you are in human form you will always be a sinner no matter what you might do or believe.

There is only one way to move beyond sin and that kicks in only after you die. It's the idea that you have to make a choice, you can accept and follow-become a slave-servant for-of a savior-god which allows you to move to heaven after you die, or reject that savior and be doomed to an eternal hell. Meaning you will either spend eternity in fiery torment or in heaven where all is good and you get to spend forever worshiping-giving energy to and being a slave of another being.

In Revelations 20, I noticed the burning in eternal hell concept seems to get cancelled. The bible says that after the second coming of Christ and Satan is defeated he will be locked up for 1000 years and then be released. Once he's released he will continue to be the bad guy so god will finally destroy him and earth. Since Satan is in charge of hell if god destroys him wouldn't that mean hell and all the souls there would be destroyed along with Satan?

It wouldn't make much sense if the god that preaches forgiveness decides to destroy Satan, also his creation and the one who supposedly corrupted man in the first place, and is behind all the evil on this world, and left man to live in hell forever. Who would he have running hell with Satan gone?

It's claimed that man has the choice to accept god's son and be saved or not accept him and go to hell.

It's claimed this decision is up to us and no one else. If you really think about it you will realize that since man is born a sinner he is already condemned to hell so his only choice is do what god wants or burn forever.

He isn't picking hell, he is already going there.

When you read the bible you will find that this god is supposed to know all, that everything is done according to his plan, and that nothing can happen that isn't his will. If this is true then he already knew what Satan was/is going to do and what he will do with Satan at the end.

This should tell you that god has already decided and knows what is going to happen to each human (book of life) before they ever get to earth and that he controls everything that happens to them while here. If this is true then man has no choice about going to heaven or hell which means this loving, forgiving god is allowing man to be created knowing full well that many of them will not accept his son and end up burning forever in hell.

God would have known that when he created Satan he would turn against him and that humans in the Garden of Eden would do what Satan wanted. It means that god knew and that it was his will that man would fall in to the trap of sin, which is also his creation. Notice the circle?

One of the interesting things about the concept of sin is that we are still held accountable for what someone did several thousand years ago. This is from-by a god that is supposed to be loving and forgiving.

He commands his followers to be forgiving, to turn the other cheek, yet he can't seem to do this for those he created, calls his children, and even sent his son to die for.

Everyone is supposed to be beholden to his son for taking away our sin, yet everybody is still being born as a sinner, so I fail to see where his death did anything for us that in the past killing a goat and giving some to this god had done.

Another point about sin is that two Christians cleaned and washed in the blood of the lamb (remember Jesus died in their place) can get married and have children that are still sinners. This is like two pure blood German shepherds mating and having poodles as puppies.

If Jesus was with his father before he came to earth in human form, knew that death was an illusion, and that after his physical body was killed he would go and be with his father, then what was his sacrifice?

Then there is the concept of the word eternal. To be eternal something would have to always have been and always will be. How can someone give you eternal life when the only way to be eternal is to already be eternal? It's a heck of a sell job to convince people someone can give-sell them something they already have, eternal life.

Another point they make is if you don't accept Jesus as savior you will burn in hell forever. How can that happen if you weren't already eternal?

You should ask yourself why would a god who knows all, created everything, including the angels and demons, good-bad, sin, karma, salvation, reincarnation, and heaven-hell, create a conflict like this.

Remember he made all the rules, and has total control over how both sides play the game, and then tells us it's our fault we have a bad life here and are going to hell.

I have to question why would we want to go back to a being that was willing to create us and stick us here to suffer and then tell us if we don't follow his rules we can't go home and will suffer forever? What's to say this god wouldn't send us to another world to suffer once we reach heaven?

REASONS FOR THE KARMA, SIN TRAP

You can trace the reason for these programs (sin-karma-religion) back to the concept that there are beings behind the scenes that live off of the energy humans produce and need us to remain within the earthly matrix so they can survive. They can continue to get this energy only by convincing us-fooling us to remain within their system. By creating the concept of religion, sin, karma, heaven and hell, and making these the default programs on this world, they have made us feel guilty and worthless over everything we think and do. This causes us to live in fear of what will happen to us here and after we die.

It makes us, our ego mind very willingly give our energy to another being we have been lead to believe we need in order to leave this world for something better. A place we already were and still are.

By creating religions based on guilt and fear these beings are able to play both sides of the game using humans as its pawns and energy source. It's a win-win for them and lose-lose for humans that accept sin or karma as truth and don't understand they can say no to both concepts. Humans stay within the system because we believe we have to and can't leave without help from some being outside of us.

I believe that sin and karma are concepts that were designed to control the thoughts and behaviors of humans on this world so we believe we have to keep coming back to this matrix. These ideas-concepts make people feel guilty about doing or thinking about anything that is outside of the programs. We are given a standard for living the prefect life that we can't ever hope to achieve while being alive so we are always going to feel less than, or worthless and will fall short of what we are told we are supposed to be.

When you are told your thoughts can condemn you what chance would you have without begging for help. It was done to create a fear-worship relationship which the creators of this system need to live. It's the fear of going to hell, or suffering while here for something you did in a past life that you don't even remember doing that keeps many people willingly standing in the submission-slave line.

Don't follow the rules and you get punished, follow the rules and you get rewarded. Isn't that the same thought pattern used by parents and our society to get kids-us to behave and do what others want?

The concept is to focus now on making someone outside of you happy so you can be happy after you die rather than being happy now thus giving others the control and power over your life.

All the channeling's, psychic readings, and past life regressions talk about how much love and caring is in the spirit world and how everyone is accepted for who they are, that there is no negativity or judgment of anyone or anything. This means there is no reward or punishment outside of what we create in our mind.

This trap keeps mankind divided by making us think that any one not living the way we are is wrong. It keeps people focused on wanting to keep a power outside of them happy and always worried they might do or say something wrong and get punished for it. It's known as the, if we can just be good enough concept.

There is no sin or karma except what we create in our minds and there is no punishment or reward. Enjoy each life for what it is and let others do the same. Get past the concept of feeling guilty or that you have to be punished, and learn to love yourself and others. Once you do that we can change how this world operates and more importantly, you will be able to leave this universe when your physical body dies without having to be reinserted in the time line and deal with this shit all over again.

CHAPTER 3

Reincarnation a matrix trap or a reality?

REINCARNATION IS JUST ANOTHER PROGRAM like sin, karma, heaven, and hell. It's designed to keep people within the earthly matrix by believing they have to return to earth until they have enough experiences or are good enough to move on. It's also designed so we accept the idea that when something bad happens to us we deserve it, hence we willingly remain unhappy and don't work to change it.

If you understand and accept the concept that past, present, and future are all happening at the same moment and that we can and are living an almost infinite number of lives all at once (within the matrix, other realities, universes, and dimensions), then there is no such thing as reincarnation. What we are really doing is shifting our point of conscious awareness from one event-life to another.

Think of all events that have ever happened and will ever happen as different videos in a huge library all of which are playing at the same time. The further back you are from the videos (higher vibration) the more videos (events-lives) you can see at one time.

As you move closer (lower vibration) the less you can see and the more focused you are on that one life.

When you take one video off the shelf you enter that event or life time and become a part of it. When you do that you can no longer see the other videos, but they are still there and still playing. Most the time our awareness is focused in-on one video, one chapter at a time (linear) within this vibration, but those beings behind the scenes are a few steps back from the videos so they can see more of them at one time.

When we finish one video, because of beliefs we have accepted while in that video, we believe we have to watch another (reincarnation) rather than being able to step back and pick what we want to do. This gives them the permission to insert us in another video of their choice.

The concept of reincarnation plays on the ego minds fear of death or non-existing. The ego mind wants to continue existing after physical death and gladly accepts the idea of reincarnation, just like it accepts religions in general, as a way of accomplishing this. Of course it is fooled because who and what we thought we were in that life isn't who we are in the next life and we usually have no memory of that prior life or having been the person we were so afraid wouldn't exist after death.

As long as we haven't remembered who and what we really are while on earth (multidimensional beings) our spirit based on the ego minds prior life memory-belief will continue to accept it has to come back here and remained trapped within this matrix.

What happens is not that we leave this body at death and are recycled-reincarnated in to another body for a next life; it's simply a purposeful-directed shifting of our conscious awareness from one life to another life that you lived at the same time.

If past, present, and future are all happening at the same time it is easy for those beings behind the scenes to shift our conscious awareness from this life to the beginning of another one that we are already living at the same time as another aspect of source-ourselves.

This is why a person sometimes see what we call future lives or events, during a past life regression. If the future wasn't happening at the same time, viewing those lives-events wouldn't be possible because there would be no memory of what hasn't happened or been decided yet.

Reincarnation is just a shifting of our conscious awareness from one point in space time to another point in space time within this matrix system. The beings in the fourth dimension (4D) trap our aspect in the astral level as it leaves the body and then shift our point of awareness to what we call a next life. This happens even if a person doesn't believe in reincarnation, but does overly attach to things or people on earth, believes in sin or karma meaning they feel guilt for anything they did during that life, or any of the other programs that keeps us on some level believing we must return.

According to the new age movement-religion the in between life concept is where we go and set up our next life. This is another program-illusion set up so people will believe-accept that after they leave this body they have to come back to another life as energy slaves without memories of who and what they really are.

The moment at or just after death experienced by people having a near death experiences in which they see their entire life flash by, is called a life review. That moment is actually where the 4D beings are scanning their minds to find out what their beliefs were-are so they can project the illusion of what they expect to see after death. This ensures they-we will head towards the light often shown in the movies, and have an experience that keeps the earthly illusion going and will make us more willing to come back to earth.

Remember you are already having all those lives-experiences at the same time and they were all set up when you entered this universe to play out all possible roles and time lines.

The reason there are so many spirits trapped within this system is the only way to break out is to understand that you are already a multidimensional being and that you are already having all your lives-experiences at the same time, and have no need of coming back time after time-life after life.

You are already being everything you are supposed to be and if you move beyond this matrix you will remember that and then can enter any of those experiences with full memory of the others. There is a chapter on escaping the matrix you can read for more details on getting out of here.

If you can accept the concept that you don't have to come back here or evolve to a higher level, then the next time you leave this world your awareness will be able to shift from focusing on one point in space time to truly being the multidimensional being you are.

This will allow you to view-experience as many points in space time as you want or enter the one you choose, not what others are picking for you.

You will move beyond the matrix veil because you will understand-know that you no longer have to be a part of this slave system unless you want to.

I believe that many of the star seeds that incarnated here for the ending of this cycle are on earth for the first time yet they still have memories of having lives on earth.

What they did is go to the akashic records and select lives to view of those who had already experienced earth in order to have a better understanding of the beliefs and limitations of this dream world.

When these lives are viewed just like in the room full of videos example, the viewer becomes part of what they are viewing, meaning they feel whatever the person who lived that life was feeling.

This life becomes imprinted upon them just like they had lived that life on earth.

Even Dolores Cannon mentioned imprinting in one of her books.

They pick many different lives in order to have an understanding of the problems connected with incarnating on earth, and they also pick lives-realities in which these problems were resolved. What this means is when they incarnate here, shift their point of awareness, they are on the fast track of experiences.

They are able to work through issues much faster and remember more than most people because they have already experienced the life-reality in which that issue was resolved and kept the memory of it within their DNA.

Also they aren't sending aspects of themselves along all the different time line possibilities like those that get stuck here because they need that energy-focus on this time line in order to change the point of awareness for all beings within this universe to a different time line.

They are here to help others at this point in space time to remember they are trapped within the system and allowing the beliefs of this system to become their true reality. These are belief systems like religion, sin, karma, reincarnation, love, having to repeat lessons, and so on. These programs keep a person believing they have to come back to earth over and over.

All of us only come to earth one time and are living all our lives here at one time. Remember past, present, future are all happening at the same time.

Don't allow the system to make you believe you have to keep coming back so they can keep you as an energy slave by shifting your awareness to different points within the time line. Understand you can leave this matrix after you leave your physical body just by believing you can and then wanting to.

What gives me the ability to do this? AFTER I leave the physical body? I take the same awareness I have while IN the body so why can't I shift to the physical BEFORE I die to the physical body?

CHAPTER 4

The of Illusion Fear.

WHAT IS FEAR? IT IS worrying about what you think might-could happen, not what is happening. You are afraid of what doesn't exist and might never exist, afraid of an illusion created in-by your ego mind.

When someone holds a gun to your head you aren't afraid of the gun, what you are afraid of is what will happen if there is a bullet in the chamber and they pull the trigger and shoot you.

Fear is a controlling illusion which is why the news always talks about what might happen and what could've happened, yes they even want you to be afraid of what didn't happen. How many times do you hear them interviewing someone after an incident that says they could've died in that incident? Since they are standing there talking with the reporter they apparently didn't die, so why should we be afraid of or worry about what didn't happen to them?

One reason is they want to create fear in humans so they can feed off that energy and control us. People in fear are much easier to control since you can play upon that fear and then provide a solution to prevent their fear from coming true so they will gladly do what you want and give up their freedoms.

Another reason they want to keep people in fear is those behind the scenes are not creators and they need us to keep this world, based on illusionary fear, existing. Without our fear energy this world as it is would fade away and so would they.

A world based on fear is where you are reactive to what goes on around you because you are afraid of what it might lead to, meaning you allow others to dictate what you create in your reality. When you react based on fear you are still controlling what reality you are in. The difference is now you are moving to the reality where the things you fear might appear, verses being in the reality you want to be in. Whatever you focus your energy-emotions on is what will appear in your reality because you will change your reality to one where your fears might come true.

Of course they don't really want your fears to come true they just want you to keep believing they might.

As long as you are living in fear you believe that your life is controlled by someone or something outside of you.

Fear is always based on what you believe can-will happen and this is always based on your beliefs and not taking responsibility for or control of your life.

When I talk about your fears being based on your belief system a good example is religions since they are an entirely fear based way of controlling people.

People are programmed to behave a certain way. If someone is practicing what they have been told a witch might do or doing healing energy work outside the church, they are told to fear this since it must be from the devil, a being they are taught to fear.

Without the church-religion telling them this was wrong they wouldn't have known, but because of what they were told and now believe, they are afraid. This is installing a fear and then using it to control.

If you grew up in a house where your mother was bitten by a dog and now has a fear of dogs because she believes she might suffer the pain of being bitten again, you will have that belief system (fear of dogs) forced in to your reality. You will grow up with a fear of being bitten until you are able to see beyond that belief and learn to accept dogs as individuals and not as a group of biting machines. You will move beyond a fear of dogs by changing your beliefs.

This is also true of the beliefs you are programmed with in religion. Once you learn to see people as individuals, understand that each one is different and that each one has to walk their own path, that your path isn't the only one to enlightenment, you will see beyond the fears religion has programmed you with. Accepting people for whom and what they are is a step in changing that fear based belief system.

Another step to get rid of fear is letting go of the belief that you need someone outside of you, a savior, to save you. Once you claim ownership of your life the fear of whether you will be good enough for that other being to save you will be gone.

Another fear based control system those in power use is reporting things (news) to make us respond in a certain way.

When the government comes out with a news story about how bad the economy is or is going to get or that another war is going to break out, they do it to create a fear response in us based on what they say might happen. They are not reporting news since these events haven't happened, yet they call this news and tell you it's their duty report it.

They are practicing fortune tellers and psychics. The very same type of people they tell you are crazy and should be avoided. They are reporting things this way to make you afraid. By being afraid of what hasn't happened, we give those possible events energy which in turn can lead to our moving to the reality where those events occur.

If they tell you the economy is going to slow down you may start cutting back on your personal spending or wait on your plans to expand your business. One person doing this isn't going to have much impact but if they can convince thousands of people to cut back they will cause a slowdown in the economy that wouldn't have happened on its own. They reported it because they wanted it to happen based on an agenda of those who will benefit from it.

By reporting one disaster pending story after another they are sucking your energy. They can't do this as much with a love base energy which is why you rarely see love based stories on the news. Remember fear is using your imagination to create something you don't want."

You are probably asking, what about death? If I don't fear it does that mean I will not die physically? No it doesn't, at least not at this point on our journey. Death of the physical body is a necessary part of coming to earth. It's a way of leaving this world when we have finished the role we came here to play.

Once you understand that death is only for the physical body, that your spirit is eternal, there is no reason to fear death. Death of the physical body is the start of a new adventure, don't fear it embrace it.

People don't have a fear of dying but a fear of losing their sense of self, of no longer existing. They fear losing the personality, who and what they think they are on this world. It's the ego mind that fears ceasing to exist since everything beyond the ego mind knows death is an illusion.

Who you are in this life and what you experience, the personality, the memories, thoughts, and feelings will always be a part of your subconscious. In actuality your life isn't real, it's a thought that source/your subconscious choose to experience in an illusionary-dream physical form.

What you will understand when you leave this dream reality is that none of those identities are who you really are, yet all of those identities are a part of who you are. It's like the saying you are everything and you are nothing.

It's only when we remember that we are eternal beings, meaning we have always been and always will be that we understand that the identity we cling to now is only a part of who we really are. It's also remembering that this reality isn't real.

When you understand and accept these concepts you will no longer have the fear of losing one's self upon death, which means the fear of death and not existing, will be gone and you can start to enjoy your experience and even look forward to the next one.

Fear and all the emotions that go along with it are some of the issues you should get under control while you are in this 3D world. When you have no fear of what someone or something can do to you, they or it can't control your reality so they or it will not control you.

The main thing to remember is that you can't die, so release that fear now and start your journey towards remembering who and what you really are. If have no fear of death, why would you fear anything else?

CHAPTER 5

Love is not answer to fixing or leaving this world.

IT IS BELIEVED BY MANY especially in the new age movement and religions that the key to fixing everything is love. If we can just love each other enough, what is known as unconditional love, the world would be great and all the problems would disappear overnight.

Religions sell-preach that their gods, saints, saviors, and leaders are all about love for their followers and we should strive to be like them. In their religious books-teachings are many stories about all the people those gods have killed or ordered killed and how their followers have suffered. These stories alone should make you wonder-question where is all the love they sell and why would we want to be like them.

We are told by the new age movement that source is nothing but unconditional love and that the beings in higher vibrations are all about love. They want us to believe that if we can just get to this higher vibration everything would be perfect.

All of this sounds just like the basic story line in all religions; you can't reach the goal they have said you need to reach while you are on this world, but when you die you can get it all, if you are good enough.

With the accepted concept that love is all you need, there are plenty of people willing to take your money and teach you how to better reach this goal, the goal you will never be able to obtain while here.

Rather than being the answer to all the problems of the universe love as we know and express it can be the most selfish, controlling emotion-feeling there is. People only do for others, show love because of how it makes them feel, and what they can gain from it.

Most the time doing what we call loving things for others, it's done because we expect the person we are doing it for to respond with the proper amount of appreciation. If we don't get the level of thank you-appreciation equal to what we did or gave, we get upset and probably don't do it again.

No matter how you look at it, love is based how it makes the person doing it feel and/or what they get in return for giving it.

Think about it this way, if every time you did something that you considered loving for someone else you got kicked in the head, how many times would you help or love others?

When people say if everyone just loved everyone else things would be great and everyone would be happy, what they really mean is they want everyone to be that way so they can get what they want and be happy. They don't want to struggle or worry anymore and they don't really care about how anyone else feels unless it will make their life better and happier.

Think about what love does to a mother or father when it comes to their children.

Love for their children makes them worry about, get angry with, and fearful of what might happen to them. Love for their family doesn't make them happy, carefree, and have a better life all it does is make them more stressed. They want their children to behave and turn out in a way that will make the parent feel good regardless of what the child wants.

If their child should die before they do then their love for that child makes them sad and unhappy for the rest of their lives.

What about the mother that kills her children before she kills herself? She loves her children so much that she doesn't want to leave them in the world to struggle after she is gone.

Some religious people claim they love their god and kill others because they believe it's what their god wants and it's a way to show their love. The Christians have done the same thing in the past and killed many in the name of love for their lord. Look at the bible and what that god did not only to his followers but to anyone who stood in the way of him or his children. He did it all in the name of love.

Think about the person who is willing to kill for the love of their county and/or life style. It's still love isn't it?

Look at all the people who want the illusionary love they see in the movies or read about in books because they believe it's what real love is.

It's the kind where they meet the eyes of someone from across the room and bells go off, they get tingly all over, and can't take their eyes off the person they are seeing.

They suddenly become a better person and their happiness knows no limits because they think they have found that special someone. What this love actually does is now give them control over the other person who would do anything for the one they love.

We feel that giving your life because of your love for others is noble. We are told that the saviors did that for their followers and of course we want to be like them.

If someone were going to hurt your child would you be willing to kill the person in order to stop them from harming your child? What if they did hurt, molest, or kill your child, would you want revenge, to make the person suffer as you are? You can't usually make them suffer as you are because you are suffering in the name of love.

Think about the guy who loves money or the politician/person who loves how power makes them feel and is willing to lie, cheat, and kill to keep what they have or get more. What about the people that would kill someone who scratches their car, steals their property, or maybe even their girlfriend/wife? These people love things the same as others love people. It's all love and it's all about how it makes them feel. People are willing to fight and kill in order to prevent someone or something from taking that feeling away from them.

This means love is not only pleasure, but pain and hurt. It can take the form of anger, jealousy, revenge, be tough or hard, as well as enjoyment, fulfilling, caring, and compassion.

Feelings of love can cause people to display all levels of emotions and feelings from feeding the homeless, killing someone for hurting their child, to killing because you want to show your god you love them. This is because love isn't a balanced emotion or feeling it's an extreme level of emotion-feeling.

Many would say these people-examples aren't doing what they do in the name of real love. That they are messed up in the head and normal people wouldn't do things like that. I would say normal people do these things every day and what they do is done in the name of love. Just because you define love differently doesn't mean you are right and that their feelings of love were-are any different-less than yours.

Love makes people behave differently, simply look at a stalker, because love is an extreme emotion and not balanced. In terms of duality love would be at one end and hate would be at the other. We think hate is bad but it is no more extreme than love is.

When people use the term love and you ask them what they mean they usually describe other feelings and emotions. Some say love is compassion, caring, trusting, others would say it's tough and hard. Ask the parent why they beat their child and they would say they love them and want them to be tough enough to face the world. People use the term love to show the extent or depth of their feelings or emotions which tells you love doesn't really exist as a separate feeling or emotion and it's something each person can describe and/or express differently.

The term unconditional love gets used a lot by the new age crowd and supposedly enlightened people.

Unconditional love means you accept the other person no matter what they do, say, or who they are. It doesn't mean you always like what they do or say but you don't judge or hold it against them. You see the spirit in them and our oneness which separates the spirit from the act/s. They say just have unconditional love for others and all will be well. That beyond us at the light level that love is all there is and if we can only get there life will be great.

This level of love is supposed to be beyond what we consider love here and something most accept that we can't achieve or really understand on this world, but all will be great when we die, leave earth, and get to this love fest.

This is the same concept as religion. Give me your faith, money, and time now and when you are dead you will get your reward of eternal life, or the ability to give-understand unconditional love. They are both goals you can't achieve while on this world which makes them different versions of the same matrix program. They're just promises so you buy into and accept their concepts now in exchange for something you will get or understand after you are dead. The money trail always leads to a program of bullshit.

There is no greater example of service to self than the feeling/emotion of love. We embrace it because it makes us feel good.

The love concept is put out there as the answer to all problems and the only path to becoming truly enlightened. Simply love yourself and others unconditionally and all will be good.

When you think that love is the only answer you are still thinking in terms of duality. That one part of something is the real answer. It's like thinking that light is the answer and you need to avoid or overcome darkness. Darkness is part of light just like hate is a part of love. They are one in the same energies and when you focus on only one part of something and avoid or feel you must overcome the other you are still living in duality, a state of unbalance. This is why people have different ideas of what love is and express it differently. It's all about levels.

Love isn't the answer to all our problems; it actually causes most of them. Love like every other emotion-feeling on this world is part of-a level of every other emotion-feeling we have. We are just taking what is one emotion (centered-balance) and breaking it down in to degrees or levels. We place terms for this one feeling-emotion on both ends of a made up scale and call them opposites, like love-hate, happy-sad, elated-depressed, sickness-health, calm-upset, attentive-distracted, and so on.

In between each of these ends are more levels as we move back and forth between the extremes.

We look at hate as the opposite of love, but doesn't a person who hates, love to some degree the feelings-energy they get when hating what they hate? You could say they love hating because of how it makes them feel. This is the same as people who experience love.

Most religious people perform acts of love for others because they are told it's what their god wants and they will be loved more.

The more good deeds they do here the more rewards they get after death. They also do many loving things in order to get other people to buy in to their religion and again get more bonus points for getting their god more energy.

Another reason for people doing loving acts is most religions make their followers feel guilt. They are told they are born sinners, losers, worthless, that even their thoughts can cause them to go to hell. If that doesn't cause guilt than I don't know what does. They figure if they can just be good enough, do enough good deeds, or pretend to love others enough they will be saved. They act as they do from guilt and fear not from love, which again places their intention purely about self gain.

Interesting how many people buy in to the idea of getting their reward after they die for what they do while alive. I have a great piece of property I can sell you now, but you can only get-use it after you die, any takers?

Ever wonder how many religious people who claim they love their god unconditionally would continue to go to church on Sunday, pray, or read their bibles if they turned on the news tomorrow and saw their god being interviewed and they-he-she-it said they would no longer be giving their followers eternal life or placing them in paradise-heaven upon death? Still think people join religions because of their deep unconditional love for a god-savior they have never met?

When it comes to the word love we seem to have a desperate need to tell others we love them and a deeper need to have them repeat it back.

The real reason we tell others we love them, is because we expect to hear those same words repeated back to us. If not we experience a large variety of emotions including confusion (maybe they didn't hear me), upset, surprised, angry, betrayed, embarrassed, and hurt. This occurs even if we have told this person we love them and they have repeated it back to us hundreds, even thousands of times before. These emotions happen even if they have shown us they love us throughout their life as in the case of our children or our parents, but suddenly didn't say I love you back to us.

We feel that love is fleeting and I think the reason for that is we know inside that love is not a balanced state of being and that anything unbalanced will sooner or later have to change position. That unless we constantly hear it expressed from the people around us (in words) it means they might have changed their minds or maybe never really loved us to start with. That the only way we can keep them telling us they love us and maybe we feel the only way to keep them loving us at all, is by us always telling them we love them.

This is also a way of using guilt to keep them saying they love you because you want to make sure they would feel bad if they decided to stop loving you because after all, you love them and they don't really want to hurt you, do they?

We also feel that if we tell someone we love them and don't hear it back, we have now given them power and control over our life and our happiness, and that causes us great fear.

We have made ourselves vulnerable because we have expressed something that is an extreme emotion, and that feeling may be beyond how they feel about us. We like them more than they like us so now they can control us by using our extreme emotion of love against us. Love is a measurement a level of our feelings just like inches and weight are measurement-gauges.

If you love someone then you love them and it should not be based on them having to repeat those words back to you or do anything. If they have to do something back its conditional love, I will love you as long as you continue to tell me you love me and constantly do things that make me feel loved.

These three words, "I love you," have become as common in usage as hi, how are you doing? They are simply said out of habit rather than from feelings. When you look at the face, the eyes, and feel the energy from a person that's really experiencing love for you, you are experiencing what love really is, a level of projected energy, not words.

Because love is an extreme emotion and not a balanced state of being we believe it can be here now and gone-changed tomorrow.

If we know they love us why do we still get upset when we don't hear it repeated back? The reason we need others to tell us they love us is so we feel we are worthy of being loved. If someone else says they love us than it means we are a good person and worthy of loving ourselves.

It comes down to our own lack of self worth, self esteem in our ego mind. We need feedback from others that we are loved in order to love ourselves.

We use the word love to express a wide range of emotions and varying depths of feelings depending on how the individual using those words defines love.

As you can see love isn't a separate emotion but a combination of other feelings-emotions rolled together to express an extreme state of being-a level. A constant state-level of love is no healthier for a person than being in a constant state of hate because they are the same, extremes.

It's the same as a pendulum on a clock that swings one way and then comes back the other way. It can't stay at either end of the swing unless held there artificially. No matter how long it is held, at some point it will break free and swing back the other way. The only place the pendulum can stay at rest is in the center-balanced just like we need to be.

I'm not saying we should never swing to the extreme ends of emotions because there are going to be points in our lives here where it's necessary and these experiences are partly why we are here. I'm just saying we don't want to stay in the extreme emotional positions that our goal should be to achieve balance.

Rather than saying you are in love or using the term love, describe what emotions or feelings you are experiencing and that will help you to become more balanced-centered in your life.

CHAPTER 6

Living in the moment real or false.

THERE HAVE BEEN A LOT of books and articles written on the subject of living in the moment. It has become widely accepted by many as the path to enlightenment, gaining truth, and understanding higher spiritual concepts. The living in the moment concept is to keep your focus on where you are at that time, enjoy what you are doing rather than spending your thought process living in the past or future. The idea is to only focus on the future or past when it's needed for something in the moment and then return your focus to the present moment.

I would like to present a little different idea that came to me on the concept of living in the moment. It is generally accepted in quantum physics and among most people who are known as metaphysical, new agers, and spiritually enlightened people that linear time as we live it is a concept that was invented for use on earth, but doesn't really exist. See the chapter on time for more details

It is generally accepted that the past, present, and future are all happening at the same time. The higher vibration you are the more of the past, present, and future (possibilities) you are able to see and understand at the same time.

You are able to see how those possibilities-choices all play out so know where each decision-path will lead. They are not separate events one after another but all playing out in the same instance. Hence the idea that time isn't real.

That is why our higher self-subconscious is able to set up the life we are now experiencing-viewing, have lived and will live, and knows exactly what we are going to do because they can see all paths-possibilities we can take.

It is also why our guides and teachers are able to help us and guide our journey because they (we) already know where we are going. This concept is covered in detail in the chapter on free will-choices. That time is not a series of events that happen one after another, but all possibilities past, present, and future are happening at the same time. This is actually the only way what we would call time travel is possible and that is another chapter in this book.

If the concept of past, present, and future (non linear time) all happening at the same time is true, than it would follow that any thought we have whether it's from our past, present, or future is being in the moment. The only difference between this moment in time and any other moment in time is simply where we have chosen to place our focus-awareness. Focusing on one moment in time is no different than focusing on any other moment because in reality they are all happening at the same instance and yet not happening at all.

On this world-dream we often chose to focus on what we are doing or where we are since we have a hard time focusing on more than one event at a time.

With the memory wipe, there will be a chapter in my next book covering this concept, we get when coming here very few people are able to consciously be present in more than one reality-moment at a time.

When you let your mind wander to past events or think about future events does that mean you are not living in the moment? No it doesn't. Any moment is a moment and you get to choose which one to focus on.

Don't feel bad because you aren't focusing on where you are right now, being in this moment because all moments are just as real. Remember they like to say this reality is an illusion and none of it is real. If that is true than why would it matter what moment you are thinking about because they are all just as real?

Enjoy where you are or what you are doing, or allow your mind to focus elsewhere from time to time; it's all the same when it comes to time.

When you are enjoying where you are or what you are doing, your focus will be there. If you aren't enjoying the moment your mind will take you to a moment you can enjoy. One of the accepted concepts is to work on being happy no matter what is going on with or around you. It's nice if that happy place happens to be that moment, but if not then why be unhappy by having to be stuck in that moment.

Change the moment by changing your thoughts. I do agree with their idea that there are two ways of dealing with things in order to be happy, accept it, or change it which can include leaving that event.

Another problem with attempting to live just in the present moment is that you are always reacting or responding to what was going on around you.

This means you are actually living in the past rather than the present moment since you're reacting to and seeing what has already happened.

Think about our nervous system and how we see things or think. No matter what you are seeing, hearing, or doing you are responding to something that has already occurred. The time it takes our eyes to take in the light, bounce it around, send it to the brain to translate and fill in the gaps, then have the thought about what it is you are seeing, what you were seeing has already passed.

New studies have shown that a part of our brain (probably area of conscience-unconscious energy connection) has already made the decision about what we are going to do several seconds before the thought reaches our awareness process and then we respond.

This shows that we are just acting out what another part of us has already decided and that living in the moment is impossible because we don't have a conscious choice. This goes back to my knowing that free will doesn't exist at our level and we are just acting out the role and choices that were designed for us in this life. You can read more about this in the chapter on free will and choice.

The moment is going to be different for you than the person sitting next to you no matter how close or aligned you are with them. It is also different from every other person or being in this dream world.

You could be watching a car race and your focus or moment is watching the lead car. For the person next to you their moment or focus could be watching the last place car or the vendor walking around selling drinks or food. What event is really in the moment, all of them! All of these things are happening at the same time along with everything else that has ever happened or will happen. This means that no matter what you are focused on at any time, you are always focused on the moment which is actually the past.

Like many other programs within the matrix, believing that you should only live in the moment and have to work to do so, is just another way of creating a religion and trapping people within one school of thought-path and making them believe this event-moment is real.

Living in the moment would be better explained as allowing your life to flow.

The best path for us is always being shown, but we are usually looking, because of living in the ego mind, to create our own path in a direction we believe we have to go no matter how many road blocks are in the way. Wanting to create our own path means we have to cut down bushes and trees, and lay out a trail to follow. We see a mountain in front of us and decide we need to go around it or make a tunnel through it, when the best path for us would've been going over the mountain.

When we allow our life to flow and follow the path already laid out for us all the hard work has been done and we can spend our time experiencing-enjoying the sights-events along the way.

This doesn't mean it will always be an easy journey, but it does mean that everything and everyone you need will be there.

Following the flow is living in the past just as much as is living in the moment because we are following the signs as they appear. With the way our human bodies are created and having to use our five senses we simply can't see anything that hasn't already appeared. There may come a time when we can move beyond the constraints of our human bodies and see more, but in order to do that we first have to believe we can.

CHAPTER 7

Worshiping the clock god! What is time, does it really exist or is it a creation of man?

Do you realize just how much are our daily lives are controlled by the concept of time and its indicator, a clock? We set the alarm in the morning to get up for work. Rush and get stressed because according to the clock we are running late. Skip breakfast or things we want to do because we don't have the time that day. Spend the day at work watching the clock so we know when to take a break, when to eat, and when to go home. If we get paid by the hour that clock determines how much money we make and how many things we can have in our lives. We get upset at traffic because according to the clock it's moving slow and it means we have less time at home to watch our television or sit and stare at the clock until it says we have to go to bed.

We get home and look at the clock to know when it's time to eat dinner or how long we have to stay hungry before we are allowed to eat, or decide it's too late for that snack before bed no matter how much we might want it.

Is it time for the show we want to watch or do we have enough time to watch a movie before bed.

How long can we talk to our friends and family on the phone before the clock says it's been too long and we need to say goodbye. How long can we play with our kids before the clock says we have to stop so they can go to bed?

On our days off we wake up and look at the clock and say it's too early to get up, or it's getting late I better get up. When we use expressions like, "I slept in this morning," we are looked at by others like wow you moved beyond the control of the clock and did what you wanted. They think I would like to do that but I'm not brave enough to deify the clock god.

We say things like it's time to eat, or it's too early to eat, it's too early for bed or it's getting late I had better get to bed.

For those that are still watching television or listening to the radio they replace the clock in another form. They entertain you until that program ends or they have a commercial, and that means you can take a break or go to bed.

Our clocks tell us when to eat, when to sleep, when we can go to the gym and how long we can stay, when to get up, when to take the dog for a walk, how much we can eat based on the time we have, how long our vacation will be and how much we can do in the day during that vacation.

It has been allowed to control every aspect of our lives and we accept it without a second thought. We don't do some of the things we want to do because the clock says we don't have enough time, or it's the wrong time of the day or night to do it.

Everything in our society operates on the clock so we can only take care of business and do many things based on certain hours of the day or night. The idea of being a slave to time means we no longer follow our inner guide about what we want to do or feel we need to do until we check with the time god to see if it is alright. Think about the times you were doing something you wanted or liked doing and you were so engrossed that you lost track of time. I bet you really enjoyed those events until you saw how much time had passed and realized the clock god wasn't happy because you had forgotten about it. Did the moment you looked at the clock take away some of the pleasure you had been feeling doing what you wanted?

We have made time and the clock that represents it a controlling god in our lives. It is a force outside of us that we allow to completely control our lives. It's like a religion in that we feel it is beyond us, something we have to obey, and something that has control over what happens in our lives and how we spend that life.

If you want to see how much you are controlled by the time-clock god do this experiment. Find a day in which you have no appointments or work, a day in which you could take a walk all day and it wouldn't matter. Cover all the clocks in your house the night before with paper so you can't see the time. This includes the clocks on your computer, phones, and every other device you have that tells the time.

From the moment you wake up the next morning keep an awareness of how many times you look at a clock to see what time it is and how you feel not being able to see it. Do you feel a slight or major panic when you wake up and can't see the time so don't know whether or not you should get up?

If you want to go back to sleep do so, if you can. During the day, eat when you are hungry without worrying about what time it is. Leave the television and radio off for a day and maybe even the computer. Take a nap if you get tired, do things you want to do without worrying about what time it is and if you'll have enough time to finish.

Take a walk and don't worry about how long you are gone, getting back to eat at a certain time or watch a show on TV. Spend the time from when you get up until you go to sleep that night enjoying yourself without breaking the day down into minutes and hours.

By the end of the day your stress level will let you know how much the clock-time god controls you. I understand people are working and letting go of time while they are working isn't something they can do and still keep their job, but wouldn't letting go of time on your days off be a nice change?

Time what is it, does it really exist or is it a creation of man?

Time is one thing, a control-limitation in our life that everyone views differently yet we all live by and perceive time as a force that controls our lives and most events on this world.

Sporting events are timed down to the hundredth of a second, space launches have to be planned ahead so they can be done at a certain time in order for the ship to reach its target when that target will be at a certain place in space, our daily and weekly work schedules are set by time, waking and sleeping patterns are mostly determined by what the clock says rather than our bodies natural rhythm, and science works with the smallest of particles that exist for a billionth of a second.

We run our lives based on minutes, hours, days, and years. We place a time frame-age on everything that exists on this world and in space around us. We even want to put an age on the universe. We attempt-want to view everything in terms of time and the older something is the more we are in awe of it.

Our lives are ruled by the concept of time yet it is something we believe we have no control over and know very little about.

Is there time outside-beyond the earth, and do alien races have time and is it different than how we perceive it?

Time is something that some within the scientific community especially in the area of quantum physics don't believe is real.

The metaphysical community believes linear time is something humans have made up-created for use on this world and other beings don't perceive time as we do. The beings that speak through channelers, claim that time doesn't exist beyond earth. They find it amusing that we have created and use something that doesn't exist.

Linear time on earth is just as real as everything else we deal with and experience on earth, which means it is something we-has been created in order for our limited minds to handle-experience so many detailed events. Could you imagine what it would be like to suddenly see-know-experience everything that has and will happen to you from birth to death with every possible path created by every possible decision you would make? What if we added in multiple lives and all those possible paths? You can see it would probably overwhelm our brains.

Time in and of itself isn't real because it was created and anything that is created has a beginning and an end. It was created when source decided it wanted to experience itself. It's not something that humans created on earth we simply keep breaking it down in to smaller and smaller moments.

We exist as we do in this moment in time, space, and awareness because at the instant the unconscious mind-source decided to experience itself on all levels at once, time was created. At that one moment in which time was created all that is was created and gone in the same thought.

At this point of dream physicality we are experiencing what source experienced in a moment of thought, as billions maybe trillions of years.

It divided itself in to aspects on an almost infinite number of levels in order to experience all that it had thought created. This is where the concept that we are all one comes from and the only level where it's actually true.

When anything is created it means time is created because all creations have a beginning and an end. Time exist no matter the distance-time is between the beginning and the end. Any thought or action involves time because they have a beginning and an end even if all those thoughts are at the same time. Any time our focus or awareness is directed towards something such as an event or life, time slows down so that point of awareness can be fully experienced.

There is an acceptance of the idea that past, present, and future are all happening at the same time, that the idea of linear time, one event happening after another, isn't real.

I can accept the idea that all events are happening at the same time, but the fact that these events are happening indicates time exist, including on other worlds and in other universes.

The difference is how time is perceived (remember it is a creation just like humans and all beings are) and this has to do with the vibration-observation-perception-dream level of those beings observing and/or participating in those events. Time as a creation is the same no matter where it is created. A life time is a life time whether it's a bug that lives for hours or a star that lives for billions of years.

I believe a way to define time is, "Time is a unit of measurement that has a beginning and an end."

It is a unit of measurement the same as length, volume, and weight. It's created to give us a standard so we can all operate on the same page. It's a unit of measurement that is the same all over the world with the only difference being how that time is perceived.

When I talk about how time is perceived I am referring to how it is viewed as passing based on how much time a being can-is perceiving and how they break it down. The smaller unit of time being focused on the more awareness of time passing-linear events that being has. The smaller the unit of time a being focuses on corresponds to an increase in stress level.

Someone whose life is based on the passing of seasons isn't going to get upset by how little or much they get done in one hour or one day yet in a medical emergency the difference between life and death can be measured in the seconds it takes for the doctor to start a procedure.

It is very difficult for us or any being-entity to perceive time beyond what we-it understand and is experiencing-living within its life time.

How it perceives time is also based on its beliefs and the limitations those beliefs impose.

Before humans started living based on clocks most people based time on the seasons rather than hours, days, or weeks. They planted food, hunted, celebrated, and collected food in different areas based on the time of the year, which is the natural rhythm-cycle that plants and animals follow.

As we have become more advanced-developed we have broken time down in to smaller increments, which increases our stress because we look at a smaller and smaller picture-window of time thus becomes more aware of its passing. It's much more stressful to be concerned with the passage of minutes and hours than it is with the passage of a season.

Humans as we are today can't really understand or perceive what it would be like living for ten thousand years any more than an insect that only lives for twenty-four hours could perceive what it would be like to live for ten years.

If an insect that only lives twenty-four hours could perceive time it would as the day turns in to night, understand its physical life-time is almost done. During its life span it would have gone from being a baby to an adult, bred, and passed in to old age all within a day, yet for it a life time has passed and that is how it would have perceived it.

To us the life of this insect is simply one day out of the thirty thousand or so days humans normally live and really means nothing to us.

Most people don't notice the passage of one day any more than the passage of any other day. For most humans the passage of a year is the first notice of time we perceive as having passed, which is why most people celebrate their birthdays and only then do they sit down and look back on what has occurred over the last year. It's then they realize the changes in their life, changes that were rarely noticed by them from day to day or month to month.

If you compared our life time to the perceived life time of a star which will be around for billions of years at our level of vibration, our existence would not be noticed by the star.

Again it comes down to the perception of the passage of time since time doesn't change and only exists because we perceive something as happening.

Here are a couple examples that might make the concept of time-events clearer. You are out walking and see a small opening-hole in the side of a hill and decide enter this opening and explore. As you enter this hole it suddenly opens in to a huge cavern filled with monitors that show you every inch of the rest of the cave system. From your position you can clearly see every monitor at the same time which means you are able to see the entire cave system at once.

The hole you entered and this cave system would be a universe and you would be your subconscious. Each of the monitors shows a different life, possibility, and event on all planets within this universe.

Now rather than just seeing the cavern on the monitors you-your subconscious decide to experience the entire cave system by sending aspects of itself-you in to every area of the cave system at the same time. Each is wearing a camera and full body sensors that relay every feeling and emotion the wearer experiences as they move through the cave system, and everything feeds back to your monitors and you.

This is what source did when it had the thought to experience itself on all levels and possibilities at once. It became the monitors in all universes in order to experience what it had created.

As your aspects leave the main cavern and move deeper in to the cave (deeper dream level what we call a lower vibration level), the caves and tunnels become smaller and narrower and there are less monitors in those areas showing the rest of the cave system and none showing the area they just came from. This would be like moving from observing the universe to observing a galaxy, then going in to the galaxy to observe a solar system, then down to a planet, and then in to a life or event.

As your aspects move deeper in to the cave system their visible world becomes only what they can see with their light and there are no more monitors showing other parts of the cave. As their light moves around their small cave what they can see becomes one scene after another just like our life on this world. We put these events-incidents in a linear fashion even thought they are individual snap shots of the whole.

It's like looking at the cave wall. You can only see the parts that your light shines on, yet the rest of the cave wall is still there. As your light moves around the cave you see it as one area after another creating a linear event-time line.

If you were to set up large lights in the cave and turn them on, rather than seeing a narrow view with your flashlight, you would now see more of the cave at one time. We are able to expand our view of this reality as we understand more about the programs of limitation and control we are focused on.

Eventually you could be in this limited area of the cave so long that you forget how you came in, that there is anything beyond what you are seeing, and how to get back out. You can only see that which your focus is on because of where you are.

Your subconscious can direct it's' aspects any way it likes in order to view-interact with different areas-events. Your view of one event-the time it takes for it to happen would be completely different than that aspect of you that is experiencing that moment because of what else you can see happening at the same time.

Think about sitting on top of a mountain and being able to see 50 miles in each direction. From your position you are able to see several towns and roads and you can see how the traffic is affecting each area at the same time. You notice that traffic is slowing down in one area and that a short distance ahead it returns to normal speed.

If you went down the mountain and got in a car on one of the roads, you would have a much narrower view of traffic and how you perceive time would change because you can no longer see ahead or the big picture. If you were stuck in that slow traffic time would slow down even more because your focus is where you are and on what you can see.

You would have no idea that traffic speeds up just a short distance ahead because you can't see it like you could on top of the mountain.

That is the difference between being at our current awareness dream-vibration level-focus and being at a higher vibration level, how many events we can see at once and how we perceive the passage of time.

I don't know why the aliens being channeled claim they don't experience time because if they exist-were created, meaning they have a beginning and an end, have thoughts, then they experience time. Their perception of it will be different than ours because of their vibration-point of awareness and how far they have travelled in to the universe-dream world.

I think that linear time does exist on other worlds (in other dreams outside of earth) they simply see more of those events at once. Remember if they have a thought or a life, that thought/life has a beginning and an end there for time exists.

I believe the deeper in to the event-dream we go the more our perception of time slows down which is why we can only deal with our life-events in a linear format. The more you move out of the event and/or from a planet, back to a galaxy, a universe, and then outside the universe, the more events-lives you can focus on at one time which changes how you perceive time.

A thought outside this universe may only be a second there, but inside the universe billions of years could have passed for those aspects of you at planetary level.

At source level, from which all that ever was, is, and will be came; all time, events, universes, and existences are only a nanosecond in time. It was a thought to experience itself from which all was created. Remember this thought came from nothing which is all that is real. Nothing became source in order to have a thought and experience itself.

I use a nanosecond of time only because it represents a segment of time much smaller than we can ever focus on.

This entire universe and all universes that are said to be billions upon billions of years old are in reality formed and gone in that one nanosecond of time-thought.

For us and other beings these universes may go on for billions of years from our perception as we shift our awareness from event to event-world to world, but in reality they were formed and gone faster than we could ever understand.

The billions of years we believe it took for our universe to form aren't real. It is only from our perception of and desire to put a time frame on everything that we have decided how much time has passed.

All the beings, races, and alien worlds that exist in this universe are actually us from-in the past, present, and future. They have not evolved beyond us because they are us played out along the time line.

Is time real? No, it is a creation just like everything else that exists and that is why we and other beings see and perceive it differently. Anything that is created has a limited life span and anything that has a limited life span isn't real.

Time was created in order for source to experience itself on an almost infinite number of levels at the same time, yet that thought and all it encompassed will be and were gone the instant it was created.

For us and our other aspects to experience that one thought of source in its completeness may take an eternity of time because there are an infinite number of universes to be experienced by our awareness. At the same time we must remember we are already those other beings and universes and the only thing that shifts is our conscious awareness of where we are in that experience.

CHAPTER 8

Time travel, possible or just another matrix program?

THERE HAVE ALWAYS BEEN MOVIES and stories of time travel, beings coming back in time to help save us, and people going back in time to change present and future events. Is any of this possible?

My feeling is no, at least in the sense of what has been shown in movies and in stories. I do believe we are able to see-visit different events or what we call different time periods but in a different way and will explain why.

Let's start with the idea of going back in time and the reasons for doing so. Most people if told they could go back or forward in time would do so for one of a few reasons. The first would be to change or prevent an event from happening in the past in order to change the outcome from that event forward. This would not only change their life but that of everyone on this world from that moment forward. An example would be stopping the assignation of President Lincoln or giving advance notice of the bombing of Pearl Harbor. Maybe killing Hitler when he was a child, or to change or prevent the death of a family member.

Maybe going forward in time to see how an important decision made now plays out so they could come back and change that decision if they didn't like the future outcome.

Others might want to go back and take advantage of a situation that they missed. Could be buying a very old baseball card when it was issued, getting a piece of land when it was cheap knowing it would become valuable in their time, or buying gold when it was selling for a few dollars an ounce. Maybe buying a painting from a very famous artist when they were first starting out, or buying certain stocks when the company went public.

These ideas have to do with a person gaining something, usually financial wealth from an event they missed out on when it happened the first time. The same would be true going in to the future to see what becomes valuable and getting it now. What they don't realize is that anything they do either in the past or future would change them and an unknown number of other people.

Another reason for going back might be to witness an event in history. Some might want to witness the birth of a religious figure or be standing in the desert outside of Roswell, New Mexico when the space ship crashes. Could be meeting someone from history just to know if they were real, or witnessing any event in history to know that it really happened and exactly how it happened, to see if our recorded history is correct. Maybe going forward in time just to see what is going to happen.

In order for the concept of time travel to be possible every moment of time, past-present-future that was created by source would have to be on a repeating loop and/or all happening at the same moment, now!

Anything else and you would never be able to witness an event that is-has happened outside of your current time frame because it wouldn't exist beyond when it happen or hasn't happened yet.

In our world once something has been done, it's over and time as we know it moves forward. Think of time passing on this world like watching live television. You can see the events in real time (in reality you see it after it happened) but once it is done the next scene is on. The only way to see the prior event again would be to have a DVR-camera to record-preserve that time frame which means you can then go back and watch it over and over again just like the first time.

One theory is that there are an infinite number of universes-realities because each decision we make or could make forms a branch universe-reality where each possible decision is played out and within each universe-realty each decision made creates more universes-realities and so on.

What actually happened is that when source had that moment of thought to experience itself, it created all possibilities and outcomes on all levels at the same time, meaning all events-experiences occurred in one instant of time and were then gone.

After reading the chapter on time you now understand that what source experienced in an instant, we are experiencing in billions even trillions of years because of the creation of time and our narrowing of focus on-to events.

Since all events occurred at the same instant we can enter any of those events-experiences-moments in past, present, or future with our awareness at any time, which is actually what we call time travel.

When you are time traveling you aren't actually going anywhere. What you are doing is moving your point of awareness from one point in space time to another point in space time. Like picking which scene you want to watch on a DVD rather than having to start at the beginning.

If you wanted to watch the creation of this universe you would just enter that point in space time and not go any deeper. Maybe billions of years would have passed at our earthly level but from where you are it would seem very quick. If you wanted to watch a certain planet form you would go deeper in to the event, and go even deeper if you wanted to watch a race of beings created, and even deeper to see a life time or a single event. The deeper you go the more time slows down because of how focused you become.

In order to watch a certain event occur on this world you would first have to find the time line-universe-reality in which it occurred and then enter that event.

If you desired to become a part of it, meaning do more than just observe it, you could, however as soon as you do your awareness would be shifted to the reality where you were already a part of it and your life would play out differently than what you had known before. Even viewing the event changes it on some level.

Entering and attempting to change an event doesn't change anything within that universe-reality-event-time line because all you are doing is shifting your awareness to the universe-time line-reality where what you did actually occurred.

Maybe those beings (us) from the future are able to follow an entire time line from beginning to end, or at least enough of it to find the point on that time line where they can enter and change their and our awareness to another time line.

What is said by different channelers of beings from other worlds is that they have traced the problems-outcomes that occurred on their world to decisions made at this point in time on this time line. They claim they have come back to help change some of the decisions made now in order to change what happened-happens on-to their worlds.

By now you understand that what they would be doing is changing-move their and our awareness from this time line-reality-universe to another one and not actually changing anything within the time line-reality-universe that they came from.

Remember all that could happen has happened it is simply a matter of moving your awareness to the universe-timeline-reality where what you wanted to have happened actually did.

I think we have moved from-shifted our awareness and theirs from what was a machine world-tech time line to a more natural spiritual time line like they wanted us to.

This of course will change the time line reality they were on to one that has a different outcome for them and us.

If they were actually changing what was happening here and now on this time line meaning they would be changing future events, they might never exist in the future depending on how those changes affected their reality. This would-could mean they would not be able to come back here and change anything which means everything would go as it was so they would then exist and could then come back.

Being able to change things within a time line-event can create an endless loop in which nothing would ever change so the only way it would work is if the changes were made to the point of awareness we both had within the time line-reality-universe. The old time line would continue on only our awareness would no longer be there.

So does time travel exist? No because all events happened at the same time. You aren't changing times in a linear manner going from present to past or future, what you are doing is changing your point of awareness to a different part of the cave.

CHAPTER 9

What is consciousness and how do we connect to it

SCIENCE HAS STUDIED THE HUMAN brain more than most other areas of the body because they believe it controls everything else yet they still don't understand it. They have spent years and large amounts of money searching for human consciousness, the subconscious and unconscious minds in an effort to locate and define these minds.

They want to know if these minds are inside the brain or body, or are they something outside the human body, more spiritual in nature?

They would also like to find human consciousness to see if they can transfer it to another body, a computer, or even a robot so that person could continue their existence on earth outside of their original body. This is known as transhumanism.

Metaphysical and spiritual people have their own ideas of what these minds are and where they are located. They like to place these minds inside the physical body within the head and heart center yet outside at the same time.

They add light bodies which are outside of and around the physical body and charkas which are inside the physical body and connected to the light bodies.

Seven is the generally accepted number of these bodies but some claim there are as many as twenty layers.

They give each layer a name such as the emotional body, and they are considered different levels of consciousness. There are lots of books you can read about the light bodies and charkas if you want to know more. Since I don't believe these layers have anything to do with our consciousness I am not going in to detail about them here.

I do believe these light bodies and charkas are programs that we accepted and/or attached to when we incarnated here. I think they are simply more layers and traps for people to get caught up in rather than understanding they are just programs that aren't needed.

The programs in this reality-matrix are layered so when a person gets through one program-layer and thinks they are finally cleared-cleaned, they soon find themselves in another layered program with more processes to go through and more money to spend in order to get cleaned-cleared again. It's designed to keep people focusing on barriers- issues rather than understanding these steps are programs designed to keep us incarnating over and over on this world. I say that because when you believe that you have to work past all these levels you will always find more of them no matter how many you clear.

This in turn keeps the belief in your brain that you haven't finished clearing all the levels needed in order to ascend, which means at some belief level you feel you have to come back here and keep going.

Unfortunately you don't get to come back and pick up where you left off, but end up getting your mind wiped so you have to start the process again. That is if the next time you are in a life that is allowed to remember-learn those levels-programs exist and that you have to clear them.

Religion gives these minds different names in an effort to maintain control over their followers so they don't stray too far from what they are being told and taught by their religions. There are books you can read about this subject so I am not going in to detail here.

The information I have received on the brain, ego mind-mind, conscious, subconscious, and unconscious is different than most schools of thought. Each of these systems has a different function yet all are interrelated-connected and necessary to each other for us to operate on-in our 3D earth.

I do not believe the brain, mind-ego mind, and what we call consciousness exist when we are not in a life form. As you read how they are connected and interact you will understand why I say they don't exist when we are not incarnated as a life form. Sometimes I will refer to the mind-ego mind as just the mind or the ego mind but I am talking about the same thing.

The brain is a computer and operates on whatever programs it receives regardless of the consequences or effect to itself or its' host-our body.

Think about the idea that our brain allows cancer to grow uncontrolled within the human body including in the brain.

If the brain cared or had an awareness of what was going on, a consciousness of its own existence, and was more than just a computer running whatever software-programs it gets, it would stop cancer and all other illness, diseases, and infections that would threaten its survival and that of its host body.

We know from studies that our body has the ability to heal itself from almost anything as evidenced by the many people that have had terminal diseases-illnesses disappear, even overnight in many cases. We also know the brain controls what goes on in the body so it has the ability to issue heal commands to our cells in any part of the body. That it doesn't always happen shows it isn't consciously aware of what it's doing to its self or the body because it has no awareness of being alive or that it can die. The brain is not consciousness nor does it contain consciousness. The brain is only doing what it's programmed to do and in our case that means it operates based on our beliefs whatever they might be and however damaging those beliefs are.

The brain accepts any programming that comes through the ego mind no matter how distorted it might be. That is why some humans can be cold blooded killers and other humans can spend their life helping others.

This programming includes everything you have ever heard, read, or watched regardless of the source. The information you receive determines your beliefs, which in turn creates what you are experiencing within your physical body.

Now you know why kids have to go to school and memorize, not learn and why the news and commercials repeat the same type of things over and over, it's all about programming our brains.

From the time you are born you are told, hear others talking about, and see pictures of people getting old. You accept this as fact and along with getting old you accept that the body will break down with things like the eyesight failing, muscles weakening, and all the other problems we are told we must go through as we appear to age. This becomes your accepted belief-program so the brain relays that information to every cell in your body and as always they follow their instructions to the letter.

This information is also contained within the default programs in our DNA and why many of us end up with family related physical problems. The information within our DNA is accepted programming from our family history, what they believed during their life.

Because of the accepted belief we must age we spend trillions of dollars and countless hours working to slow down this process never really believing we can stop it or have more than a small chance of slowing it down temporarily.

Occasionally you will hear a story of an old monk who never appeared to age beyond a certain point and died looking much younger than his given age.

Most would believe this isn't something they could do and that the monk must have spent years learning whatever he learned to stop or slow down the aging process, or it was in his family DNA. It is in the DNA because the DNA contains and is our beliefs.

When he changed his belief to one that he didn't have to age he changed his DNA, which changed his body. Their belief-programming that they can't stop the aging process is the reason they can't.

Of course those behind the scene use the ego minds vanity about getting old and ugly and its fear of not existing-death to their advantage by producing products and systems we will buy and follow in an effort to slow down a process we don't believe we can slow down or stop.

The entire medical system is based on the ego minds fear of death and its desire to stay alive as long as possible. Think about the trillions of dollars spent in the effort to keep people alive and the treatments they are willing to undergo in a desire for one more day.

What's the difference between a martial artist who has trained himself so he can be hit with a sword and not get cut and your average person? They are both human with all the same parts made from the same cells yet one can perform something almost everyone would consider impossible.

How about the person who lifts a car that weights several thousand pounds off a family member yet at the gym they would be hard pressed to lift their own body weight?

The only difference between the people performing what is considered impossible and those that don't do these things, is the belief within the brain and what it's telling our body it can or can't do.

The person who lifts the car overcomes their belief of what they can do (limits) because the stress of the moment over rode their belief system if only for a short time.

The martial artist has spent years working on his mind so he can overcome the accepted believe that a person has to be cut when hit with a sharp metal blade. Change the programming in the brain and you can change or remove your limitations. Especially when you understand none of it is real.

Let's look at the ego mind which is the loading program for all information that enters the brain including the automated basic programming contained within the cells-DNA. It doesn't matter whether the information comes from the world around us through our five senses or from the sub-conscious (spirit world) through the conscious mind.

The ego mind is the only place where we have an awareness-sense of separation, and an awareness of nonexistence (fear of death).

The mind is our default program for how all information we hear, see, and read is sent-programmed to the brain. Since the ego mind is also where fear is created all information is filtered through the emotion of fear and the ego which is how the mind views itself-us. The ego views itself as the physical form and believes that's what it really is hence the ego view of us-itself is not always based on facts, reality, or how others see us.

Our ego will twist and enhance things that happen in order to look-seem better. It hates to be wrong and will argue, fight, and lie in order to ensure-feel it is right.

Remember what the ego is in your life and you will understand how all information-beliefs that it programs in to the brain are tainted-filtered.

The information most people are being programmed with is what the powers to be want programmed in to their brain, giving those in power the ability to control and limit what we think we are and can become. It's also how they get us to buy their products and accept their programming on what is important and what we should worry about. That is, worry about what hasn't happened (fear). All programming on this world is designed to target the ego mind and keep as much control over humans as possible.

The ego mind is the voice you hear talking and in some cases yelling, in your head when it comes to worry, fear, hurt feelings, anger, and those types of emotions and feelings.

It's the part of us that wants to be accepted, loved, be noticed, always be right, gain material possessions, power, status, fame, and so on. It wants these things because it believes the programming being sent by those running the show that these things are what is important and real. It also judges others and itself based on these ideas.

The ego believes having the right address or brand named clothing changes it-us and a lack of those things means we are nothing.

This is the programming it accepts from the world around us and where it gains its sense of identity.

It's in the ego mind that religion is based-accepted since that is where the sense of separation is created.

The ego mind is not designed to remember a connection to spirit or source as our consciousness is so it doesn't remember that connection is always there and there is no separation.

As long as the ego looks outside of itself for everything including being saved, it will be controlled by the programs of this world and religious control over people will remain strong.

The ego mind is necessary for programming the brain and is always present when spirit is in physical form. The difference between worlds-beings is how much control the ego mind is given and how much the life is lived-programmed through the conscious mind rather than the filters of the ego mind.

I believe that everything created-built-made by man on this world is a program-vibration that is designed so it will be seen in a certain way and that determines how we react to those programs-things. Your thoughts-beliefs on how your body will react to different foods are a good example of programs you have accepted.

One day we are told a certain food is good for us and the next month told it's bad for us. Most the time our beliefs change to follow what we have been told even though all food is made from the same energy-atoms.

These are default programs that we automatically accept as long as we are unaware they exist, and that we can say no to them, that is change our belief programs by living through the subconscious conscious connection rather than the ego mind. These programs are the beliefs we accept because it is what we see and are told is true.

Everything in the physical realm is designed to be translated by the mind so the truths often remain covered.

The only place fear lives is in the ego mind which has knowledge of self and a fear of non-existing, thus all information loaded in to the brain is tainted by this view, based on how it will hurt or help its survival.

In reality everything that exists including us is made from the same things atoms, energy, and vibration all of which were created by source so it could experience a physical reality. When you understand this you realize your body is no different than the chair you are sitting it in, or the car you are driving. It's the ego that gives us a sense of separation from everything else.

The conscious mind is the bridge between our subconscious mind and the ego mind, spirit and physical worlds.

The subconscious is our spirit guides-teachers, that aspect of us that is outside this physical realm. We are aspects of our spirit guides. They stayed outside the physical but still within this universe in order to assist us. They can see what we are doing and know all that is coming so are able to guide us to where we need to be.

The subconscious mind is our intuition, what we tap in to when we listen to our inner self.

You access this information-feeling through the conscious mind which bridges the gap between this physical realm and the spirit realm. There is an awareness of existence at the conscious level but no fear of death or a sense of separation because of its direct connection to the subconscious.

Through this connection the conscious mind knows death is an illusion and that we are always connected to source, our higher self.

When you truly start letting the conscious mind filter the programming to your brain you will move beyond the need for religions, the desire-need to follow the path of others, and the idea of anything being above or beyond you. You will remember your direct connection to source and be able to move beyond the default programs-world of fear the ego mind and this world lives in and be able to start exchanging the beliefs-limitations of this world for the freedoms of truth.

The consciousness center or connection point within the physical body would be at the heart center but is not a physical thing that can be trapped or transferred to another body. The only aspect of human awareness that could be caught and transferred would be the information programmed in to the brain. This information for most people is from the ego mind so you could say they would also be transferring the ego mind, but the ego mind isn't a physical presence so they would just be transferring its energy-programming.

At this point I don't know for sure if they were to transfer the brain to another body, computer, or robot if it would still maintain the conscious-subconscious connection, but my feeling is no.

Remember the ego mind is the only part of us that believes the physical body and this life are real and all there is.

Transferring that aspect of us to another body or computer would not help us advance spiritually it would only serve to enforce the limiting beliefs we already have.

Consciousness is not something that has to be cleared or cleaned because that bridge is always connected and open for us to use. The only thing you have to do to connect to your sub conscious and step beyond the ego mind filters, is be aware that you have the connection and start listening.

Just by believing it is there you have already started reprogramming your brain to accept different information. Once you do that you can start to move beyond the ego mind-this worlds programming and began to change the beliefs in your brain which will help you to change realities, hence your life.

As I said before the subconscious mind is actually an aspect of us that has stayed beyond-outside the physical realm and is connected to all aspects of us-it within this universe at the same time.

We are programmed to think and believe that anything beyond this 3D world has to be better, know more, or be more advanced than us, which is why we use terms like guides, teachers, ascended masters, and light beings.

This is our limited thinking caused by the ego mind, programs here, and believing that who we think we are is all that we are. Simply put these guides and teachers are us!

When you are allowing our life to flow rather than trying to control everything with your expectations of how things should be and go, you are allowing the subconscious mind to direct-run things through the conscious mind.

When this happens it is the conscious mind that is programming the brain through the ego mind loading program but without the ego mind fear filters.

By allowing our conscious mind to direct our programming-changing beliefs we access who and what we are without limitation. I think this will allow us to access other areas of our brain that in turn allows us to make changes within the body consciously and quickly.

Science says we only use 10% of our brain which maybe all the ego-mind is allowed to have access to. That 10% access would consist of basic functions and not much beyond that. To move beyond that 10% we need to allow the conscious mind to determine what programs are loaded through the ego mind to the brain without the fear based-limiting beliefs-filters of the ego mind doing the programming.

Our experiences on earth are based on whether we allow the ego mind or the consciousness mind to be in charge of what information is being loaded in to the brain.

One important thing to understand is that if you don't choose where this information is received from (subconscious or ego mind-matrix), than the ego mind is the default system running and loading the brain through its filters. It's also the operating system that is targeted by all the programs of control and limitation because the ego mind is easiest to affect.

Its fear based programming that allows a few hundred people in Washington D.C. to control the 360 million in the U.S. and a couple thousand to control over 7 billion people.

The unconscious mind is what I call source. I don't use the word god any more when referring to source because the word god means different things to different people as you read in the first chapter.

Most people when they say god mean a being beyond and above them. I do not believe there is anything above or beyond us because source is us and we are source. We are simply an aspect of source experiencing itself in this reality-dream.

The unconscious mind-source is aware of and part of all that exist in all creations at the same time. Our sub-conscious mind is connected to the unconscious mind and is an aspect of it thus has access to all knowledge. The unconscious mind is connected to all aspects of itself in all universes, galaxies, solar systems, planets, and everything beyond and in between. In other words all that is!

It could be that every time source has a thought to experience itself a different way, new universes are created as well as new beings.

Other levels-programs are created within levels such as light bodies, charkas, dimensions, ect in order for source to challenge itself and see how far in to the dream reality it could go before aspects of itself got lost in the dream world and believed it was real.

I believe we are now at that level when I look around and see how many people are lost, believe this world and life are real, and all there is. Even religion-heaven or whatever you wish to call paradise is still just an extension of this dream world program.

I can't at this time say whether source had more than one thought or whether that one thought created all that is.

I know that if source had a thought even if it was all at one time, it had a beginning and an end. This means everything we know and that is, will at some point end.

Remember nothing that is created is real because at some point it will be gone, and nothing that is real can ever go away.

When we allow our consciousness, subconscious, and unconscious to take their rightful place in the process, to control our lives and direct information to the brain, we will begin getting information about things beyond our physical world. We will be open to and enter whatever doors we should go through. The consciousness as it interacts with the subconscious is able to see beyond our limitations of time and see the big picture.

Following our subconscious allows our lives to flow with a natural rhythm rather than an ego mind controlled life where we want to force things on our terms and time frame.

Allowing your conscious and subconscious to guide-run-direct the experience gives you a life where you follow your intuition and are guided to events making contact with all the people you need to contact. Your life will flow fairly smoothly because it's being directed from beyond the earthly matrix programs of limitation and control. Remember that if you haven't taken back your power-place as creator-co-creator within this dream you will not have the life flow you could have because you still believe you are a slave-servant of the system and the system will treat you as such.

There will be issues in your life from time to time simply because we are living in a physical world-body that is constantly being bombed with programs of control and limitations. At times we will allow the ego mind to step up and take temporary control. The more awake you become the less often this happens and usually for a shorter time. The conscious level is the gateway for all aspects of us.

This might be a bit different from what you have read before since many believe consciousness is all there is when we are not in physical form. To me consciousness is just the energetic connection between the physical world and the spirit world. What many refer to as consciousness I would call awareness.

My goal in this chapter was to explain how many levels there are even through they are all actually one level and explain why when we are not in physical form we have no need for any of them.

At source level there is no sense of separation, death, or individuals, we are simply one in nothing

CHAPTER 10

Ownership of the Matrix, take back your power as creators.

TAKE BACK YOUR POWER AND control, and reenter the Matrix as an owner-creator rather than as a victim-slave-servant of the system.

We have started 2015 with a slightly different idea about dealing with the earthly matrix. In the past I and many others have been looking to raise our vibration and move beyond the system, to overcome it, leave, and not be a slave-subject-servant of or to its rules-limitations-controls and laws. The thinking was we have to move beyond the physical limitations of this earthly body and leave this system to advance.

This year I received the feeling-insight that just getting out-leaving the system isn't the approach we need to take in order to complete our journey here and leave this universe for good. We realized and accepted that we are in the physical realm with physical bodies and within this matrix system because this is where we choose to be at this point in space time, thus where we need to be. This is a system that we helped create, thus are co-owners of rather than servants or slaves of.

By thinking and wanting to overcome and move beyond this system we are fighting-resisting the very system we helped to create.

We are resisting a part of ourselves and making our journey harder, thus making the system we want to leave even stronger.

We now realize that we need to move back in to the system but in a different way. We are doing it by reclaiming our true status as owner and creators, and making changes from within the system. We can do this by using the rules and laws that we agreed to before we came here until such time that we can change or move beyond them.

Rather than viewing ourselves as servants or slaves of this system and believing that those running the system are above or beyond us, we are choosing to accept our part in co-creating this system and step up and forward as co-owners-creators accepting all the rights and privileges that are part of this position.

Once we understand and accepted our status as co-owners we can move forward and make changes because our mental attitude is going to be one of a creator rather than a servant or victim.

I'm not saying we need to do the things those behind the scenes are doing when it comes to being evil to others, but we can use the same rules and laws they are using to control us, in order to make changes and let them know we are reclaiming our rights, privileges, status, and that we don't fear them.

Remember they are running this matrix as they are because we asked them to do so and on some level they are us.

One of the things Irina and I have done to reclaim our spiritual freedom is to reclaim the church that is within our body from the priestly cast that had laid claim to it from the day we were born.

Yes, the day you are born you become a corporation within the system. Your parents gave you a name and registered it with the state just like is done with a corporation. You unknowingly accept that name and are taught to believe that you are in fact that name and corporation. Because you believe you are the corporation and not just a representative of it they hold you accountable and extort money from you your entire life. You are in fact traded like stock among those running the show and are the real source of value on this world.

I am not going in to a lot of details on this subject in this book because there is a lot of information about it on line and I have not received any information from my higher self that would change the information already out there. You would have to read through what is written and decide what works for you.

The religious system and those at the head of the churches are running the programs on this world and they are setting the rules and laws to their advantage. The legal supposed separation of church and state was done for a reason, and it wasn't done in the name of religious freedom but to give the church more power and not be subject to many of the rules and laws they pass for the rest of the population. I say supposed separation because they are run by the same group behind the scenes.

Many people think the proclaimed spiritual leaders of this world are above and beyond us, somehow better people and closer to god than we are so we allow them to get away with this practice. By thinking they are above us we have allowed them to own our spiritual and thus our physical bodies.

We had already taken our spiritual bodies back in the verbal sense, but felt something more was needed because the system on this world wouldn't know what we had done according to their rules. After listening to what others have done we decided to use the system to reclaim our spiritual bodies by becoming ordained pastors.

By doing so within the system and having it legally recorded we have told the priestly cast we are no longer one of their servants, but are now their equal, back to being co-owners of this system. We have reclaimed our physical and spiritual bodies and let them know we are working with and supporting the creator of this universe and reclaiming our roles as co-creators.

We didn't do this to follow or create a religion, teach the bible, or open a church. We did this to tell the matrix we are no longer going to be their servants being tossed back and forth by the system. We reclaimed our position as co-creators in a way they would understand and now have all the rights and privileges they have given themselves.

We aren't saying that everyone needs to do it this way because I am sure there are many paths to reclaiming your role as co-creators.

Each of you will need to find a way that works for you, but all of you need to reclaim your spiritual and physical bodies or you will forever be owned by and servants of the system.

Another way I am reclaiming my power is by doing a lot of talking (changing beliefs) to my mind in order to change my body, that is get it working as it should be and not as our matrix enforced belief system tells us it has to.

I'll explain this. From all the reading I have done, listening to speakers who have had different spiritual experiences, and things that have come to me I have come to realize that everything on this world is a program designed to hold us down and keep us thinking-believing in ways the matrix wants us to in order to keep the system going.

Many have talked about us being a spirit having a human experience, how powerful the spirit and our soul are, the incredible healing powers our mind has over our body, and our ability to do anything. These same people will then turn around and say how much we are physically affected by this world with all the additives that are in our foods, polluted air and water, chem.-trails, stress, sin, karma, and virtually everything else on this world.

If we are as powerful as it is believed, than how can any of those things affect us unless we believe they will? From the time we are little we are told what we can and can't do and how things will affect us on this world.

We are told germs are everywhere and that viruses are just waiting to mutate and attack us.

We are told what the odds are we will get certain illnesses and by what age we should expect it.

There are hundreds of ads and fund raisers for different diseases and the numbers of how many people die from them are headline stories.

You should ask yourself, why is this information being placed in public view so often? Who or what gains from more people believing this information?

The other day I was called by a fund raiser for the diabetes foundation. They claimed they didn't want money but wanted me to hand out cards telling people to get checked by their doctors to see if they had diabetes.

She said there are over 5 million people out there that don't know they have it. They say they want people who have it to get treated.

If the people don't know they have it than it means they are probably feeling good which means they don't need treatment. So why would they want to get 5 million people started on their treatment programs? After all they claim there is no cure for it and no matter what treatment people get they will die from it or a complication from it and before that time may go blind and lose parts of their hands or feet. The simple reason our society wants more people to get treated for any disease is money. The sooner they get them believing they are having problems and in the medical system the more money that can be made.

It will also boost how much money the foundations are able to suck from people because the more people that are told they have a disease, the more friends and family that can be tapped to give money to fight against it.

Think about what they tell us on how foods are going to affect our body and what we should and shouldn't eat.

If you can remember more often than not the foods we are told we should eat changes from time to time and you will notice their recommendations always relate to new products that just happen to be reaching the market about that time.

They push the new product for a while and write articles about how this food, a new pill or supplement has been shown to help prevent or cure a certain problem. These stories are actually ads for their new products. Once the demand has peaked, they will come out with something else that people should take and the cycle keeps repeating.

They say it's because new research has shown something different. If that is the case then the first research must not have been very good. If the first group of people didn't do a very good job on their research and this second group is basically the same type of people trained the same way as the first group, why should we believe their research results are any better than the first group?

Look at what you believe and why you believe it. Are the beliefs you have yours, or ones your family, friends, or society has given you? You can't change a belief until you understand why you have been holding on to it in the first place. Make sure any beliefs you have are ones you want which will get rid of a lot of programs in your brain.

CHAPTER 11

Gaining freedom from the Matrix.

THERE ARE SEVERAL IDEAS AND concepts floating around about how a person-spirit can leave this earthly dream matrix and what it takes to do so. These concepts are usually religious or metaphysical in nature which on the surface may seem to be completely different, but when they are looked at closely you realize both concepts have more in common than people realize.

The new age movement which is looked at as being metaphysical is simply an expanded version of religion designed to give people the illusion of greater choice. It encompasses more open truths than basic religion in order to catch those who know there is more going on than standard religions admit, but aren't ready to give up the external god-being concept.

I define a concept as religious any time you have to follow a program with designed steps, rules, rituals, or things that have to be done in order to get to the desired end. When you **have to** follow someone else or their path you are part of a religion. It doesn't always mean the god you are following is the same one those in church are talking about.

You can follow others teachings for a time and not get caught up in it as a religion as long as you understand their teachings are only part of the answer.

You should look at everything they say-teach based on how it feels inside of you and understand that at some point, if you really are seeking the truth, you will have to leave their path and follow your own.

When you claim a title, the name of a group or organization, or want to classify-identify yourself by a certain label you have just limited how far you can grow. If you claim to be a Baptist or atheist you are bound by the beliefs of those two groups otherwise you can't call yourself by those labels. Grow or change your beliefs and now you are no longer a part of them. I would suggest you think a long time before you accept any label and ask yourself why you have such a need to belong to any group or be called by a certain title.

There are religious concepts which usually tell a person they can't do it alone because they aren't good enough and need some kind of savior-teacher to pull them from this world, or to move forward in their spiritual growth. This process usually includes the person giving-pledging themselves to this savior-being-god-teacher and following their rules otherwise you end up in a place like hell. It a give us your time and money (energy) now and someone else will give you your reward after you die concept.

Some religions believe that everything you do comes back to you and you are stuck in an endless cycle-circle of repeating or paying for what you had done in a past life.

In the chapter on Karma I talk about this process being a circle which is never ending thus a person has no way to get out of here without outside help, meaning it is just another trap.

The new age movement which is a combination of different expanded religious beliefs, thinks you have come here to work through different problems and steps in order to experience all you wanted to learn. That each time you come here you want to work on something different or finish a lesson you didn't do right the last time. It's the concept you must have been and done everything before you can move to a higher vibration and start the process again at that level.

They also believe that beings outside of them like ascended masters, spirits, and higher vibration beings are needed to help them achieve their higher vibration so they can leave this world for a better one. It's not an escape it's just moving to a different and of course, a supposedly better level of being. Unfortunately it keeps you in this same matrix just at a different level. Like religions, going to a better place only kicks in only after you leave this earthly body.

Because they believe you plan to experience being everything on every level on this world, and all the different ways you can experience each of those things, you are going to be coming back here as a slave for a long, long time.

It's believed you have to work your way up to higher vibration levels so you can get out of here and then have to repeat the process in another universe.

Within the new age religion are plenty of different ways for you to work on making your vibration higher, clearing your charkas, light bodies, and many other program layers to keep you from believing you are done and can leave this system.

Of course each of these steps-processes comes with a price tag and someone willing to show you how to do it their way for the right price. Each claim their system is the right one just like all the other religions out there.

There are a couple things all of these groups have in common for helping them to leave this world. One is the idea that if only everyone had love for one another and followed their steps this world would be a great place. If you could just love others enough you will raise your vibration high enough to leave this world and enter a place of pure love and joy. Having read the chapter on what love is you now understand that it isn't the answer or a way out of here.

Another common concept involves people in a tunnel and seeing a light at the far end after they die. Because they are a bit disoriented right after leaving the physical body they often head towards the light since it can be the only thing they see, and is the default programming of this world.

Most people have heard about heading toward the light after they die and movies often show this as the correct path for people to take. Watching these movies and accepting it as correct enforces this idea within our belief system.

Anyone who left this world thinking they haven't finished something here, are too attached to someone or something, believe in sin or karma, accept any type of religious programming about a savior-god like being or a being that is above or beyond them will automatically go towards the light and be recycled to the earthly matrix. If they hesitate or have doubts there are usually family members, angels, a god like presence, or whatever that person needs to convince them heading towards the light is correct.

If people leave this world believing they have to ascend to higher levels in order to work their way out of this system, they will be recycled within the synthetic cosmic matrix which is another layer of this system.

So how can you leave this matrix? Is it even possible when your physical body dies or is your spirit trapped forever? Are any of the processes being taught correct and is ascending or raising your vibration the only way to get out of the matrix?

At one time I brought in to the ascending process and that I needed to raise my vibration and move to a higher dimension after I left earth. I now know the concept-idea of ascending was just a step in the learning-remembering process to help me let go of those limiting beliefs.

Everything we do in this life is a step towards something else and helping us to remember more of the truth. Because we have so many, so deeply ingrained limiting and controlling beliefs we usually have to work on letting them go in stages rather than all at one time.

The important thing to remember is that none of these steps are going to be the final one so don't accept them as such otherwise you wouldn't have the desire to keep moving forward and remembering more. Always understand that what you know now may change tomorrow or next month if you are really searching for truth. Do not accept that the ideas you have now are the end all answers.

I know that even with all the information I have received-remembered it is only laying the ground work for what is to follow.

They are aware that some humans know-feel that they have to-need to leave this earthly matrix. In order to keep these people from exploring those feelings and remembering they can leave the entire synthetic universe, they added all these different levels a person has to, can go through in order to keep them happy yet still keep them within the same system. This is known as the cosmic matrix rather than the earthly matrix.

This is the same thing that happened to the first churches as some of their people decided they didn't want to follow all the rules or didn't like the people running the church, so they decided to break away and start their own church but with some different rules-ideas.

This process is continuing today which are why there are so many different types of churches even within the same denomination.

As a side note, that process alone should tell you that religion-god isn't the one true path-answer otherwise they would all be on the same page.

This process was allowed and continues because it keeps people within the religious programming framework, yet satisfies their desire to do something a bit different.

The information I received about how to leave this earthly matrix also involves leaving the universal cosmic matrix because they are one in the same.

All the other beings both on and off world, you have ever heard about and those we haven't heard about are aspects of us from our past, present, and future. All these worlds-lives are happening at the same time and are different dream levels-experiences within this universe.

The earthly matrix is the deepest dream level with the most amount of limiting beliefs and controls. We came to this level to see how deep we could go within the dreams before we got totally lost and accepted this dream as reality.

What happens on this level determines what happens to the other aspects of us on all the other worlds-levels in this universe.

Once we wake up and understand this reality isn't real and almost all the information we have been programmed to believe, isn't true, we will be able to bring all aspects of us back together and leave this universe and rejoin our subconscious or unconscious self.

To leave this world we have to change our belief from one of having to move to higher levels, go to heaven, get rid of the guilt, feeling less than, and all the others ideas-programs-beliefs that are keeping us here, to one that we can and will upon leaving this physical body leave this entire universe.

We will not follow the light no matter who asks us to go with them or what we may see.

You can't believe that you have to go to any other levels, realities, planets, or worlds within this universe or you will recycle back here and start the remembering process again.

If you want to be free from this system decide that now and work it in to your belief so when you leave your physical body you do not have to pass go and start over again.

Freeing yourself from this system will allow you to decide where your next journey will take you, rather than letting a default program make that choice for you.

CHAPTER 12

Do we have free will and choice or have we been lied to again?

WE ARE TOLD THAT HUMANS have free will and that no one has a right to interfere with our free will. The idea that we have free will-choice in our life seems to be a concept that most people accept without a second thought. They believe it to be true because every day they are faced with having to make choices and really believe they have the ability or free will to do what they want. The idea we have free will is an accepted part of religion and the metaphysical teachings.

People walk out a door and think because they can go left, right, straight ahead, stand there, or even go back the way they just came from, that means they have free will to choose. When stepping out the door do you have the free will to go straight up or down? What about going in any direction you want? What if you step outside and there is a building in front of you or a wall to your right that would make going those directions impossible? Your free will to choose a direction has now been limited even more.

Your beliefs also limit your free will because of what you believe you can and can't do.

Think back on your life and you will remember it was filled with others telling-teaching you what you can't-shouldn't do, and to accept theirs or societies limitations on your choices.

They don't tell you they are limiting your choices, you simply accept those are your only choices and anything beyond that is not acceptable or impossible. That's what science is all about, telling us what we can and can't do as humans, giving us limits.

Often times the boundaries of our choices are enforced by negative consequences. This occurs if we exercise the concept of free will to a greater degree and make a choice outside what the powers to be and society desire us to make. You have the ability to make a choice that will lead to negative consequences, but most people don't like making choices that lead to pain, more problems, or being confined in a place where you have almost no free will.

Is the ability to make a choice when those choices are limited, come with boundaries, or negative consequences really considered free will? If we are only able to make one choice-pick one, is that really considered free will?

The more I learn-remember the more I believe that free will doesn't exist on earth and what we have is nothing more than a limited illusion of choice. This system was set up so people would believe they have free will and not fight against those running the show. I guess you could call what we have as limited free will, but is limited free will really free will?

What the question, "do humans have free will," really comes down to has nothing to do with any system on earth, it has to do with whether we came to this world with our life plan and all decisions already decided by our subconscious (spirit)?

Are we only here to experience the choices already made before incarnating, meaning we have no choice in anything, or do we have an unlimited number of paths and outcomes we can follow with each path determined by the choices we make here?

Did our higher self only script the perfect plan and allow our ego mind the choice to follow that plan, or has nothing about our time here been determined and we make all the choices once we get here, creating our reality as we go, leaving everything random and to chance?

Let's take a look at these ideas and see how they would affect our life-choices on this world.

If our higher self only laid out the perfect life plan, what we really wanted to experience (in this dream), would we have the ability to change that plan or even disregard it entirely, or are we simply experiencing that plan with no choice in the matter?

If we set up the prefect life based on what we wanted to experience and everything we do is predetermined by that plan than we have no free will or choice. Every decision and choice was made before we came here and we are just experiencing those choices.

This would mean every event, sickness, accident, illness, person you meet, change in life or thoughts, is already set and there is nothing you can change about it.

You can't help but make the decisions you are making and there are no wrong choices because you are following a script like an actor in a movie.

If that is true than maybe the reason we came here without much memory of what we really are or our purpose in being here, is if you re-membered the life-experiences you had planned to live when you came here, it would defeat the purpose of experiencing it in physical form since you would know what was coming and what you were supposed to do.

Even the illusion of choice would be gone and it would be a very unemotional-unfeeling and disappointing life with everything being known ahead of time.

One of the first questions people would ask about the idea of every-thing being planned ahead of time and us having no choice, is does it means we aren't really responsible for anything we do?

That people killing each other, our corrupt government officials and systems, being beat up, raped, abused, rich-poor, sick-healthy, are just things they-we wanted to happen-experience. Is there anything we should attempt to do about it and is there any reason to get involved in what goes on in the world around you? Should we just sit back, focus on ourselves, and allow things to happen because there is nothing we can do about what is happening to us or anybody else. In a sense that could be true if you only looked at the very small picture.

Many of the new age religious ideas are based indirectly on this concept.

They figure everyone is having their own experience so you should just allow others to do their thing and not judge them or work to stop them from harming others.

Those being harmed must have asked to be harmed before they came here so allow them their experience. This again could be true if you only looked at the small picture view.

I think many people here are being harmed because they have been fed half truths and a fear based diet which means they are projecting these fears and in turn causing themselves to shift to those realities. I also think that many of the stories about the things being done to people are created and that many of the stories about humans suffering are actually simulations (sims) which are artificial intelligence (A.I.) computer or subconscious generated illusions designed to get us to focus our energy-belief a certain way and give them control over our thought patterns.

The new age movement promotes the idea that if people just think happy thoughts and don't let negativity in to their lives it will go away and not be a part of their reality. That everyone around them is experiencing just what they wanted and needed to experience, so don't do anything for anyone else otherwise you will take away from their experience.

These lines of thought actually contains two concepts which are opposite of each other. First they think everything going on was planned so there is nothing they can do to change their lives or anyone else's.

The second is that by thinking happy thoughts they can change their reality. If they can change their reality than it could mean nothing is set and life here is a crap shoot based entirely on what a person is thinking. Everything is random and chance, there is no plan and you can do what you want.

The idea of changing your reality does tie in to the concept that those behind the screen want to influence the masses in order to cause them to create the reality those in power are wanting.

One school of thought is there are an almost infinite number of realities based on every possible decision and outcome we could have so changing your thoughts will move you to another reality that is more in line with your thoughts. Don't deal with negativity or evil just change your thoughts and you will move to where it isn't happening.

The idea of sitting back and not doing anything is designed to make money off people by teaching them to focus only on self and enjoying whatever they can in life, don't try and help anyone, be out for #1, get your piece of the pie, and screw anybody who gets in your way or needs anything. It's also designed to separate and divide people which will make them easier to control.

Looking at that small picture view people could say we shouldn't have jails or a court system since everyone is only doing what they have to and no one should be held accountable for what they do.

If you look at a bigger picture you would see that the jails and the court system would also be part of what they wanted to experience and are needed so they can complete their life-experience.

Since they would've come here knowing that they would end up in jail or prison it means they wanted to follow that path and end up where they are.

When you look at the bigger picture you will see that everyone is doing what they planned to do and that they can't do anything else. There is no right or wrong decisions and no mistakes. Helping others and thinking you have free will to choose and change things are all part of the big picture. If people hide their head in the sand then that is what they planned to do until they realized it accomplishes nothing.

If we don't have to follow our prior plan does each decision create a different time line, universe, reality, outcome, or do all choices or paths we can take eventually end up back on this timeline with only one predetermined outcome?

If we can change realities and/or time lines than were all those other possible paths-realities already known and planned for ahead of time? If so this would mean every possible path was already known and that we aren't doing anything that wasn't expected and planned for. It also means all the different people we would have to connect with in order to meet at a certain time and place based on each decision we made, would have to be created-set up ahead of time or we would be changing realities all the time to line up with the person we needed to see based on the decision we just made. If you look at the scale of planning it would take to set up every possible outcome for every possible decision, you can understand why this would have to be done before we incarnated in to physical form.

If every life path is based on each decision we make while here, it means our higher self already knows we would stray from the perfect plan and all the possible paths we could take based on every outcome to every decision we could make. This would create an almost infinite number of paths we could follow once here. Would all these paths have a different ending or would at some point each of them come back to only one ending-time line?

There is one school of thought that each time we leave the physical body we simply transfer our awareness to the same us only in another life path-reality and keep going without knowing we died.

Interesting idea but at some point we would run out of us-life paths to transfer to and then what would happen. This idea doesn't seem to take in to account other roles we would be playing?

If all these different paths were seen before we came here then it would mean we aren't doing anything that wasn't already known and we could've built in lessons on those other paths that would point us in the direction we really wanted to go. There is the possibility that each time we change life paths we are working on different experiences if each timeline-path has its own ending.

What if we have complete free will and nothing is planned before we come here and everything we do is up to us?

If nothing is planned it would mean everything that happens is created by the decisions we make. If we go left one thing happens, if we go right another thing happens and no one on this world or the spirit world knows what will happen ahead of time.

It would mean there is luck, chance meetings, random events, and shit just happens. When we say, "I almost died in that accident," that was the truth and it was only a sudden changed decision, a random event, or a chance happening that changed the outcome. What happened to us would have nothing to do with gods' plan, angles, spirit guides, or our dead family members because they would have no ability to help us since we would be in full control of what happens.

Anything they did would interfere with the concept of free will. It would also mean anything we do to help another unless they asked us would be wrong. We would be interfering with their free will, with their decision making process. Why would we have spirit guides or angels if no one knew what we were going to do? It would mean religion is completely made up (which it is) because the god they are worshiping and praying to isn't in control of anything since we are making all the decisions.

This would give our ego mind full control over what we do and experience while on earth. Our spirit self would just be in the background observing and not have anything to do with our life while we are here.

In a way we would have no direction to our life and may never learn anything while in human form. There would be no reason to pick our parents or a certain body if once we got here everything was random. It could also mean there is nothing beyond this physical life, no spirit world, and we only get one chance to live. Once we are dead we are dead and that is all she wrote.

It would mean what we have heard and many have experienced in relation to god, the spirit world, our spirit guides, spirit teachers, and angles being here to help us would be wrong. We would be on our own and could expect no help from anyone on this world or another because it's hard to help someone after they have already done something and helping them unless asked would violate their freewill.

What I feel is the truth is based on what I learned and saw during past life regressions, visiting the spirit world, seeing spirits, information that came to me when I asked questions, reading books and articles, listening to others, and talking to those who are able to receive messages from the spirit worlds like psychics, and mediums. I take all that information and see how it relates to each other and then go with what feels right to me.

Even what I know now will change as I get new information just as the information in this booked changed as I was writing it.

My feeling is that once we were created as an aspect of source that we became individual beings (aware) in order to experience the completeness of that thought on all levels and all possibilities.

Source created an almost infinite number of aspects, what I call our subconscious mind, of itself and each of those aspects created a universe. They then created aspects of themselves in order to move deeper in to the layers of that thought in order to experience each layer to completeness. We see ourselves now as humans but we are just one aspect of an aspect of an aspect and so on.

As an example when source created the subconscious aspect that today my awareness calls Ron Fellion that subconscious aspect of source did not know itself as Ron but knew that an aspect of it was created on our 3D earth that is known as Ron Fellion in order to play a certain role/s. The subconscious knows all aspects of itself at the same time but isn't known as any of them.

Because all possibilities of everything already exist, we are not experiencing anything that wasn't already seen in that one thought.

We were given the role-experiences we are having so we can experience each role on all levels in these physical realities. I think this is done in each universe that was created which fits with the concept that we are already on every level of everything at the same time. I feel we may even have similar roles in each universe we enter. We aren't individuals seeking and needing to be everything in every universe because we are all part of source and are playing roles in the experience source created.

Think of source as the writer of a movie and we are the actors, with the subconscious playing the director. As an actor we are playing one role and because there are other actors we don't need to play every role or experience everything in order for the movie to be completed.

Within this universe we were given the role/s to play which includes our life on-in other worlds, dimensions, and realities. In other words all we are going to do, the roles we are going to play, in this universe was already chosen when source created aspects of itself for the first time.

This does not mean there is only one aspect of us in this universe. More than likely there is an almost infinite number of each of us in this universe active in every possible reality created by every possible decision we could've made in order to experience all levels-roles to their fullness.

Our awareness in this 3D realm may only be in one place at a time even though all those other realities are happening as well. In other words as you are reading this book this is the only place within all the 3D realities in this universe that your awareness is because of our limited ability to perceive more.

As you make different decisions you are moving to other realities in which the decision you made is playing out. At the same time the reality you just shifted from is continuing on in order for that decision-role to play out.

You might say than we do have free will since we can choose the reality we go to based on the decision we just made. I would say no you don't because that reality was already there no matter what choice you made and you are only making the choices you were supposed to make.

In other words you are just shifting your awareness to a different realty-point in space time, seeing a different scene, but you are not doing anything or making any choices that haven't already been made. You are just becoming aware of those other realities-choices you are experiencing, not creating them.

Our subconscious has already decided the roles we are (going to) experiencing in this universe and as we shift to those realities-choices our awareness moves-focuses there.

We don't actually move to another reality, we simply change our point of focus-view. It's like looking at a mountain range and focusing on one peak at a time. The other peaks are still there it's just your focus hasn't shifted to them. You aren't moving to view or create them you are just seeing-becoming aware of them in a given order just like your decisions and changing realities.

The realities-choices we experience have already been decided and done. We are just experiencing those choices with our shifting awareness.

To us it may seem like we have choices and free will since we decide what we are going to eat, where we are going on vacation, and who we are going to talk with, ect., but in reality we are limited in our choices by the roles we have picked and don't have the free will to do anything we want. There are a limited number of paths you can take because of your role and where you end up has already been decided.

There are two ways we can live these roles and most the time we switch between them until we realize how much easier one way is than the other.

One is allowing the ego mind to be in control, wanting to make things go our way, control each decision and the steps involved in order to reach the outcome we desire.

With this role we are fighting against the flow because we want to force the outcome no matter what happens around us or the doors that close to us. We say, "I am not going to do that because I want this to happen my way."

This life is very emotional with lots of road blocks, and frustrations as we work to control the path we really have no control over. Yes there are many people that follow this path their entire lives and never discover the 2nd and easier path to follow, but I think that is the role they were supposed to experience.

The second way is going with the flow, allowing our subconscious mind to direct us to the places, events, and people we are supposed to be, deal with, and meet. This is using your intuition, feeling what needs to be done. You watch for the path and directions that are presented rather than attempting to force open a door that is closed and your life seems to flow much easier and is more enjoyable.

Because of the roles we are going to play our parents, family members, friends, our body, strengths and weakness are already decided along all time lines before we come here. The generally accepted idea is we get to pick all these things before each life and decide what we are going to work on or do while here. People buy this idea because a part of them remembers that our lives are planned out ahead of time.

In a way that is true but it's another example of how a truth was twisted in order to redirect us and give the powers to be more control over what we think we know.

The decisions were made by source when it created aspects of itself and is not something we do in between lives because there isn't an in between life time and the choice isn't ours.

The generally accepted idea of reincarnation by the new age people is that you get to pick your life, family, friends, and experiences before you come here while in the between life stage. They trap people in to thinking-expecting they need the in between life stage to plan out their next life which allows us to be reinserted in to the time line and used as energy slaves.

One of the things I have been told by several different people is that I have taken on the role I am playing here, on many other worlds and it's the role I play in this universe. Now that I have received the above information on how this works what they told me makes sense. Whether I am doing the same type of thing in other universes I don't know at this point. Maybe each universe requires us to play a different role depending on what that universe is set up to experience.

It is accepted that we come back with the same spirits, known as our soul group, in each life. That we play different roles, husband-wife-man-woman-father-mother-child-friend, ect each time we come back together. No matter where we are on the world we are visiting, we usually end up together or in contact and help each other. Our soul group may actually be aspects of us playing different roles in order to help each other.

I can accept this idea based on the experiences I have had meeting certain people in this life and our feeling of already knowing each other the first time we met. As of this writing I am not sure whether we are aspects of the same subconscious or aspects from a different subconscious working together.

So how does all this fit with the idea that we don't have choice or free will on earth?

If you can accept the idea that source created aspects of itself in order to experience what it had thought and those aspects created other aspects in order to experience that thought to the deepest level possible, then you will see that everything we are doing was seen and created, and that we are just experiencing it in physical form. That everything we are doing was and is already happening and we are experiencing it with the illusion of choice and free will in order to play out the emotions and feelings involved with each decision and role.

I will give you some examples that happened in my life which will show why I believe we don't have free will and we are acting out, experiencing the choices that had already been made.

On July 19, 2012 I had a heart attack and spent 5 days in the hospital. According to their testing I lost about one half of my heart efficiency. I had believed before this happened that I had moved beyond any heart issues that I had in the past. I knew my prior heart issues were due to a closed heart towards others and it took something like heart issues to make me understand and deal with this issue.

It was about 6 weeks after the heart attack that I was feeling rather depressed and was wondering if I had gotten so far off my life path that I was not going to end up accomplishing anything that I came here to do. I will point out that at that time in my life I still had the belief we did the between life thing and picked what we came here to do.

I was feeling like I didn't want to help anyone anymore and wasn't going to write any more papers. I was going to let the people learn for themselves rather than passing on information I was getting. I was looking forward leaving this world and going back to what I believed was my home in the Pleiades.

One morning while out walking, I had a heart to heart, spirit to spirit talk with my guide and told her that I needed a sign one way or the other otherwise I was done. I say she because that is the form she has taken when I have seen her.

Later that morning we got a phone call from a guy that was interested in buying one of our baby goats. He had called the week before and had planned to pick it up then, but it didn't work out because he ended up spending more time than he planned to at another location so had to cancel meeting us.

He called that morning and said he was going to be in the eastern part of the state in the afternoon and wanted to pick up the goat. Since he was coming from the western part of the state I agreed to meet him in a town about 40 miles south of where we live.

After his call we headed out and met him just south of that town and gave him the goat. On the way back thru that town I got a feeling that we needed to stop at the thrift store.

I had been driving thru this town for 5 years and had never stopped at the thrift store before. We found the thrift store and went inside.

Within a couple of minutes I saw a lady named Shelly that I had done some energy work on several months before.

A few months before our meeting in the thrift store she called me and said that during a meditation she was told to come and see me for a session. Interesting enough she isn't the first person that has told me that over the last few years. We had a good session and I had received some information about her before the session that turned out to be correct.

The day we met at the thrift store she had come to her massage office which is located in the same building as the thrift store but around the corner. I had never been to her massage place so didn't know this when we met at the thrift store. She said she had been sitting at home that morning and was told she needed to go to her office a half hour early.

Shelly is one of those people who follow her inner self so she headed for her office when told to do so. She figured she would do some paperwork with the extra time but when she sat down to start it, she was told to go to the thrift store now. She did and we met.

Since both of us knew this wasn't a chance meeting, that everything is done for a reason I set up a massage-energy session with her for another day. I knew this was the sign I had asked my guide for that morning.

This is an example where both of us received messages to do something so we would meet. In order for this to happen the guy who wanted our goat had to call that morning and want to pick it up that day at that approx time. He was coming from the western side of the state so the timing was even more amazing.

I had to agree to meet him south of that town and Shelly had to come to work early the same day and follow what she was told to do by her inner self, and I had to decide to stop at the thrift store.

Look at the events that had to be set up-happen ahead of time by someone who knew what was going to be happening. Our meeting him the week before had to be cancelled so we could meet with Shelly on a certain date and time, and dropping off the goat was simply a way of getting us down there on that date and time.

These were not conscience decisions-choices we made ahead of time so someone else had set this up. I believe this is where the spirit guides come in and they (us) were the ones putting the messages in Shelly and my head that day so we would meet. I think the guy coming to our part of the state that day and wanting to pick up the goat, and her coming to work early and having no clients at that time were set up before and we were just experiencing-following through on the choices that had already been made.

You could say well either one of you could've ignored the messages you were getting and not ended up meeting at the thrift store. My response is no we could not have.

That is what we were supposed to do and each of us was at a point in our lives where we were following our inner instinct so this is how it had been set up. This has happened many times to me so I know it isn't chance.

When people say you could have not done something or done something else they are always wrong because you did what you did and it could not have been done any other way since you can only make one choice. Was there a reality created where we didn't listen, probably, but that wasn't the experience chosen for us to shift our awareness to.

When I had my session with Shelly she told me I had been thinking about leaving this world. I had the heart attack 7 weeks prior and had not told her about it or my talk with my spirit guide before our meeting at the thrift store. Another lady told a friend of mine the same thing about me prior to my having the heart attack.

A couple of weeks after meeting Shelly I was telling this story to a friend of mine that lives in Idaho. He then told me that a couple months before, when he was talking to Debbie a medium in Sand Point about his father she told him that his father was trying to decide if he wanted to stay in this world. She then told him that she was only going to tell him something because she knew that he and I were good friends and she didn't want him to freak out if it happened.

She said that Ron was also thinking about leaving this world. Their conversation happened about a month before I had the heart attack.

If we are making the decisions here and creating our reality as we go then how could someone know what was going to happen to me? They couldn't unless the future had already happened and we were just living the experience we had chosen.

I was feeling good before the heart attack and was looking forward to doing a holistic show in Spokane that was scheduled for 2 days after I had the heart attack. I had no idea something was going to happen to me and had no conscience desire to leave this world before the heart attack.

She knew something was going to happen to me and that I might die. If we make the decisions while on this world than there was no way she would know that since it wasn't a decision I was planning on making and it hadn't happened yet.

This is another incident that shows our life decision was made by our higher self before it happens and not being made by us here.

This example took place in 2013 and shows how we're directed to where we need to be in order to take care of problems and to help others that need us when we are willing to listen.

I was taking a trip from Washington State to Oregon and California to visit family and was driving my pickup truck. I had left my nephews in Chico, CA and was on my way to Santa Cruz, CA to see more of the family.

As I was leaving Chico I noticed that my clutch started having problems. Since it had just started happening and after that glitch it seemed to be ok, I kept heading south.

By the time I had almost gotten to Sacramento, CA and pulled in to get gas, my clutch was almost gone and the only way to stop the vehicle was to stall it out. It was a standard transmission so stepping on the brake without the disengaging the clutch (which wouldn't disengage) will make the vehicle stall out and stop.

I was able to get fuel and realized I had a decision to make. Since I couldn't stop without having to stall out the vehicle it would make it very hard to stop anytime I had to get off the freeway or slow down. It was also Saturday evening and there wouldn't be any shops open for me to get repairs, especially in a town where I knew no one.

I decided to turn around and head north since I could stay on the freeway and not have to stop for or go through busy towns for a couple hundred miles.

I drove for a couple hours and since it was getting late and I was getting tired, I knew I needed to stop for the night. I also realized it had to be a town where I could get a room near the freeway and a big enough town that I could find a shop to fix my truck.

I felt the need to take the second exit in the town of Redding, CA and was able to exit the freeway along a frontage road to my right that had several hotels. The frontage road allowed me to reach the hotel area without having to stop at any traffic lights or stop signs.

I pulled in to a hotel and with stalling out the vehicle a couple of times I was able to get it parked in parking spot in front of a room.

Without my saying anything to the clerk about what room I wanted, they gave me the room that was directly in front of where I had parked my truck.

Sunday morning I started looking through the phone book for a shop where I could get the truck fixed on Monday. I called my father in Oregon since he has worked on many vehicles and might give me a better idea of what needed to be done to my truck.

He said my brother who lives in Santa Cruz, CA just happened to be on his way to Oregon that morning to visit them and he would be passing by Redding that afternoon. I called my brother and he said he would stop by and take a look at it. He stopped by the hotel and decided my clutch was completely shot and that it would have to be replaced.

He then mentioned that he thought our former neighbors from Santa Cruz where I had lived 38 years before, lived in Redding and owned a transmission shop.

I looked them up on face book and found the brother who had lived next to us when we were kids. I sent him a face book message telling him where I was and what had happened and asked him to call me. He called me later that day and told me they still owned the transmission shop and that it was about 2 miles from my hotel. He said if I got my truck towed to their shop in the morning he would get it fixed for me.

I did that and met their father who still ran the shop they had opened over 37 years before and he recognized me.

Later that morning I was sitting in the shop waiting room to see how long it was going to take to get the parts and everything fixed when a lady walked in that looked familiar. It turned out she was his sister and when I said hi she recognized me.

She said it was interesting we had met since she only comes in to the shop to help with paperwork a couple times a month for a few hours a day. I told her everything happens for a reason and our meeting wasn't an accident. She agreed.

We talked for awhile and I realized she had an interest in metaphysical concepts and she said she had been asking to meet someone she could talk to who would be able to answer her questions.

I now knew part of the reason I had ended up stopping in Redding was to help answer her questions. I have always said I would talk with anybody that I could help, all I asked was that my guides get me to where I was needed.

When you look at all the things that happened in order to get me there to talk with her and get my truck fixed, you will realize it was all set up outside of this physical realm. That the only part I played was a willingness to listen to my inner feelings and follow the doors that were opened for me.

I also knew when it happened that the problem with my truck was for a reason and I was looking forward to finding out what it was. I don't look at problems or issues in my life as bad luck and say why me, I know it all happens for a reason and I accept that.

The idea that I could end up stopping in a town where my neighbors from 38 years before were living and that they owned a shop that happened to be the one needed to fixed the problem I was having with my truck, that my brother was going to be driving past where I was staying when I needed help and that he remembered that they live in that town and had a transmission shop, and that Brenda (the sister) happen to come in to the shop that day and had been wanting to talk with someone about metaphysical questions she was having, and you will understand that our life is directed and control outside of our present awareness, and that we are just living out decisions already made.

I would like to relate a story that involves a much longer time frame than the ones I just shared to show how things can be lined up without our conscious awareness and that the actions we take are part of a predetermined plan.

In 2009 we decided to get a female German shepherd puppy and ended up getting her through a breeder that lived about 65 miles south of us. Since she was a pure breed dog we talked about letting her have one litter when she was older just so she could have that experience, not because we wanted to get in to the puppy business.

When she was about one year old we started looking around for a male German shepherd puppy. We talked with the breeder we had gotten our female from and she said she had a male she would sell us. I decided that if we were meant to get a male puppy that it would work out and we would get one for free.

About 2 weeks later the same breeder called us and said she had a friend who was also a German shepherd breeder and her friend owed her a male puppy. Her friend currently had 2 male puppies but our breeder didn't have room for another male dog so if we wanted the puppy we could go pick it up. She only asked that she be allowed one of the puppies from our litter. We agreed since this is what we had been asking for and were receiving a $1500 puppy for free.

When the time came to pick up the puppy we decided we would make a quick trip south (about an hour drive) and then come home since the puppy had never been away from its family and it would be its first time in a vehicle.

Before we left I felt I needed to take some of the energy healing crystals I used in session with people and Irina decided to take a metaphysical book we had picked up for a dollar at the thrift store, but already had a copy of. She doesn't normally take a book to read and I don't usually take my crystals when we go some place.

When we got to the breeders house and met her it wasn't long before we started talking about metaphysical ideas and that her friend (the other breeder) had told her I had done some energy work for her.

Rather than the quick trip we planned on, we stayed at her house about one and a half hours and I Did some energy work on her sore knee using my crystals, and Irina gave her the book she had brought because it dealt with what we had talked about.

We then knew why we had decided to bring these items with us.

Before leaving I decided we should go to Costco in Spokane (about a half hour further south) and get the food the puppy was familiar with rather than heading straight home like we had planned. At Costco I went in and got the dog food while Irina stayed outside and played with the puppy. When I came out she told me the puppy had fleas. I decided we should head south to Petco and look for some flea shampoo rather than north to a Wal-Mart that would've been on our way home.

At Petco Irina decided to carry the puppy in the store while I looked around for flea shampoo.

While there I found out you can't use flea shampoo on a puppy under 12 weeks old because it can damage their nervous system.

While Irina was walking around the store a lady came over and said she owned a German shepherd. Irina noticed she was wearing some crystal jewelry so they started talking about the crystals. When she told Irina that she did Reiki (a form of energy work) and that she was looking for someone who knew rainbow energy work, Irina told her she needed to talk with me because some people have seen rainbow colored energy coming out the end of my fingers when I am working on people.

I went over to talk with her and as we talked both of us felt chills going up and down our bodies.

It turned out she was working for a dog food company and was only at Petco two days a week for a few hours at a time.

To shorten the story I ended up doing some energy work for her and her husband and at that time she told me she was being told she needed to get me on her table for a session.

That session proved to be very intense. I saw and felt a great many things including being able to stop breathing and leave my body twice.

There was more that went on but the point of this story is what had to happen and the time frame involved in order for me to end up on her table and have the experience that I did, all without my planning or knowing what was coming.

We had to get a female German shepherd a year before and decide to breed her. Rather than buying a male dog we were given one and had to pick it up on a day that Barb would to be working at Petco.

We had to bring our crystals and a book with us and stay at the breeders' house for an hour and a half in order to ensure we ended up at Petco when Barb was working. I had to decide to go to Costco rather than head home as planned, the puppy had to have fleas, and we had to head south to Petco rather than north towards home when we found out the puppy had fleas.

Irina had to be carrying the puppy around in the store and Barb had to own a German shepherd so she would be interested in coming over to see our puppy and talk with Irina. Barb had to be an energy worker and looking for someone to help her with a certain type of energy work.

All this was so I would meet Barb and we could do some energy work for each other.

By the way when we got home that night Irina gave the puppy a bath in warm water without any soap and all the fleas were gone. There weren't any fleas in the bath water after she washed him. This is an example of what is going on behind the scenes and how our lives are being directed so we can have the experiences we are supposed to have.

When people say well I make choices all the time and when I want things I usually end up getting them so it means I am making the choices and creating things in my life. I say the reason that happens is because it has already happened and you making that choice and wanting those things is because those things and choices were going to happen, and not the other way around.

No we don't have free will or choice on this world, it is all an illusion. We are just making the conscious decisions about what is already going to happen so we can experience it happening. We are not creating it or causing that reality, it's the other way around. Remember we are here to experience the choices, roles, and decisions we have already made.

Does the idea we are here to experience the decisions we have already made mean we just sit back and let others suffer, not caring what goes on in the world around us? I think for some people the answer will be yes, but for most of us the answer would be no.

We should follow what we feel inside and if helping others is what we feel is right, or we decide to get involved helping to change the world, or in stopping others from being hurt, than that is what we should do.

Don't do it because you think a false god will bless you for it. Does it because you really feel inside it is what you should do.

Learn to relax and let your life flow because you have already worked out the answer to any problems you are going to have. When something happens don't say oh poor me, accept responsibility for what is happening and know that a part of you is controlling and directing you to what you need in order to take care of your issue.

One last thing to think about if you still think you have free will and the ability to choose. If you could change anything about your life or yourself right now meaning have, be, or do anything you want, what would it be and would you do it? If you answered yes and still think you have free will and choice, how come what you wanted hasn't happened yet?

CHAPTER 13

Dream Reality, the truth about this world and all that is.

I HAD AN EXPERIENCE IN April 2015 that showed me the following concepts as being true. Physicality is not real on any level. Reality is not real on any level. The only thing that is real is nothing!

In the beginning there was darkness (nothing) and that is all there is. Everything beyond that is a state of thought-dreaming-creation-illusion-not real and at some point will end.

The experience that led me to this concept was similar to a lucid dream, yet because of how it played out and how I felt afterwards I believe it was something more. I also say this because of other experiences where I have left our reality and I know how my body felt when I returned again.

A lucid dream is a state of dream in which you become aware within the dream that you are dreaming and realize you are the creator of the dream reality and can do whatever you want in the dream. I have read some people can have these dreams at will and decide what they want to do within the dream before they go to sleep. At the lucid dream level you aren't really asleep yet not awake either.

During the dream you notice things that don't fit or wouldn't work in our normal world and you see much clearer detail. People usually wake up after a lucid dream and remember what they had done and felt. The biggest thing is you have a heightened awareness of the dream reality and know that you are in control of what happens.

I have had dreams in the past where I knew I was dreaming but I didn't have as much awareness as I did in this experience. Interesting enough I was told something like this would happen less than a month before this experience by an energy worker in Las Vegas, NV named Patrick.

He said I was going to start having more intense experiences than I have had and that the information I would be getting-remembering would be at levels beyond any I had received before. He was more right than either of us could've imagined.

The reasons I believe I had more than a lucid dream is because from the time I laid down to awakening was approx three hours and yet I only remember parts of the dream. I also know that I was only allowed to remember what I needed at that time since we never get more information than we can handle or need.

When I woke up my stomach and head felt like I had motion sickness, my head hurt, and my whole body felt like I had just come out of anesthesia at the hospital. I could hardly stand up and when I walked it was a slow shuffle with legs spread wide apart for stability. My wife said my eyes and face looked like I was wasted.

I thought maybe I needed grounding to rebalance my body so had my wife help me outside so I could stand barefoot in the grass. It seemed to help some but I was still wasted for an hour or so and didn't feel normal until later that evening.

I have had other experiences where it has taken up to 3 days before I felt normal although none were as intense as this one. When I have these types of experiences they tend to be short and very intense, like I am getting an entire lesson at once rather than slowly over days or months like most people.

I will share the parts of that experience that apply to this chapter.

When I realized I was dreaming and in control of what could happen I decided I wanted to follow the tunnel of light that people with near death experiences talk about seeing and those who have past life regression often see. My intention was to see if there was anyone really there or whether what a person sees is based on what they believe at the time of death.

I had done past life regression and did not see either the between life world or the tunnel of light that others talk about. This told me two things, one that it wasn't real and two that this is my first time incarnating on earth so I haven't gotten caught up in the trap the in between life or near death experience visions entails.

Those programs are a way of keeping people in the reincarnation cycle and the longer a being has been here the deeper in the trap they fall.

The metaphysical idea is going to the light will cause you to become trapped and reincarnate you back to this reality.

I had no fear of this happening because I knew I was the creator of this reality and I don't have to come back here unless I want to.

When I entered this tunnel of light I saw it was much brighter at the end in front of me so I started walking-drifting-floating that way. I had no feeling of moving yet the lighted end was getting closer to me. I know now that nothing was actually moving, that it was just a projection-impression of movement since everything that exists is in one location; that movement, space, and time are all creations and there for not real.

I looked around to see if there was anything or anyone, but the tunnel and lit end were empty except for the light. As I sensed myself moving towards the light to see what was beyond it, I suddenly found myself out of the tunnel and light and in a gray darkness where there was nothing. When I say I was suddenly out of the tunnel I didn't get to the end and go through, it was more like I was suddenly pulled up and out of the tunnel.

I was in a gray darkness and there was no movement, no light, no sound, no vibration, and nobody. I had a sense of being there and observing but at the same time knew I could not be a part of that darkness and still observe it.

I realized I was beyond source and at the only thing that was real and it was nothing. I had visited source before and was able to feel the power and energy that was it so I knew this was not source.

Since that time I have come to understand that this nothing is what created source so that it could experience itself.

I will have a chapter in my second book going in to more detail about this concept.

I had a sense of being there and at the same time understanding that nothing is all that was real, that everything else is a creation, illusion, an experience of self all based on a thought.

There wasn't even a sense of size, how far it extended, it was simply everything with no sense of being beyond where it was, yet there was nothing beyond it.

Another part of the dream that I remember showed me that our beliefs are our limitations in our dreams and in our lives on earth.

When I realized I was the creator of the dream reality and could do whatever I wanted, I decided I could go through a cement wall. This wasn't a thought as we normally have where we put one word after another until we complete the thought, it was a thought that I could go through a cement wall and the wall was suddenly in front of me, and I was moving towards the wall at the same time. It wasn't walking or running more like gliding or floating but without a feeling of movement. I met the wall and was surprised when I wasn't able to go all the way through it. It was more like being inside a balloon and when I pushed my hands against it would move and stretch but did not break.

At the same time I knew that the reason I didn't get all the way through the wall was that somewhere in my brain I still had the belief that I couldn't go through it, that I as a human couldn't go through a cement wall.

I had three of those types of experiences in the dream where I was shown how my beliefs were affecting my dream reality, but I think this one experience explains it well enough.

I realized it was my limiting beliefs that were controlling what I could do in my dreams and on earth. It showed me how powerful our beliefs were and that they affected all our other dream worlds. This effect goes both ways meaning our beliefs in those other dreams can affect us on this world if we chose to use them that way.

I realized that in order to change our earth dream and manifest things faster we have to let go of our limiting beliefs in this dream world.

One way we can do this is by working to reprogram our brain using the conscious subconscious connection which has no limiting beliefs, rather than using the default ego mind which believes all the lies we have accepted on this world. By being open to new ideas and doing things that we may not have believed possible before, we will start using this connection and the reprogramming process.

Some examples would be reading and learning about energy healers, tuning forks, taking herbs, and other metaphysical-natural modalities you might not have considered before.

Reading about and talking with people who have had experiences outside of what would be considered normal reality. Just doing things like these can start changing the limiting beliefs we have and strengthen our use of the conscious subconscious connect to unlimited possibilities.

What might be the hardest concept for many to accept is the idea that physicality is not real. This includes the earth, the sun, planets, stars, universes and everything we think is contained within them like humans, spirits, light, vibrations, alien beings, energy, other realities, dimensions, frequencies, and yes even light beings, and light bodies aren't real. Existence in and of itself isn't real in the way we think of things being real.

There are no higher dimensions, lower dimensions, ascending, descending, and evolving beyond the physical body. Light and spirit bodies are no more real than the physical body. You never go anywhere beyond where you are right now. All dimensions, realities, vibrations, worlds, and universes are in one place, right where you are.

Think about when you are day dreaming about a vacation you went on. In your mind you can experience the smells, feelings, sights, and be there but you are never moving outside of your mind. You are just shifting your awareness from where you are to where you want to be.

Nothing exists outside of or beyond you and never has. Space, time, and distance are illusions they are part of the dream reality as is your physical body.

You are already whatever you want to be and where ever you want to go because all is a dream world and the only limitation to what we can do is our beliefs.

We are told everything is vibration-energy and that what's real. That everything is made of different vibrations and once you tune in to them you will see what is real. The truth is it doesn't matter what vibration you tune in to because everything is a creation as is the vibration itself.

Energy, vibration, atoms, and light were all created in order for us to experience different realities in a physical form but they aren't any more real than we are. Source is light, vibration, and energy, so that it could create the physical and spiritual worlds, but source is a creation as well.

Being real, think about what that means and what something would have to be in order to be real. If it is real it would always be, meaning it would never disappear or no longer exist. How can something that is real cease to exist at any point and still be considered real? Would you say it used to be real but now it's gone and still think of it as real? The only part of it that is real is in your mind.

This is the same whether it's a bug that lives for a day or a universe that expands for billions of years and then collapses upon itself or explodes and disappears. Anything that has a beginning and an end will always fade away and can't be real.

Everything is a dream, there are only different levels of dreams (really only one level), but they are still only dreams that we can shift our awareness to.

All these different realities, other beings, and worlds are just dreams we enter with different belief systems about what we can do (limitations) on the worlds in these dreams.

It is our beliefs that limit us on this and other worlds and in these dreams. We are not creating this reality since all that is already exists within our sub-conscious; we are just limiting our awareness-access to all that is by the beliefs we are choosing to accept.

We can shift our awareness from one reality-dream to another and there are many that think we do this millions of times each day.

Imagine everything that was, is, and will be as an almost infinite number of rooms in a house. You walk in to this house, go to one room and decide that you can't leave that room. All the other rooms are still there and the only thing that keeps you from exploring them is the belief you can't leave the room you are in.

Earth is a room and all the programs of limitation and the beliefs we accept are what keep us in this room. Our beliefs build the walls around us and the more we accept these limiting beliefs the more walls we build and the smaller our room becomes. Remove the limiting beliefs and all the walls between the rooms will disappear.

We are being programmed even while in the womb about what we can and can't do and the limits of our dream world.

If you watch the news, read news papers, books, look at what we are taught in school, and almost everything we hear or see is telling us what we can't do, that anything beyond what they tell us is impossible. I call science, **"The religion of limitation"**. It tells us what has to happen and why we can't do certain things (limitation).

Miracles happens because a limiting belief system was let go even if just for a moment, or changed to the level that allowed what we would consider impossible to be possible.

When we read stories and watch movies about being able to fly, having super powers, visiting other worlds or realms, they are called fantasy or science fiction because we are programmed to think we can't do these things or visit those places.

They are just as real as this world and the only thing stopping us from being a part of those dreams is an awareness-acceptance of the belief we can't.

Every universe is a dream construct and within that universe are other dreams called galaxies, solar systems, planets, and life. Each of these dream levels were constructed with a certain belief system of limitations.

If you were to consciously enter the dream of a 5th dimension planet you would not go in with the belief you needed a physical body, could get sick, or even die. You would go in and take on the belief system set up by the creator of that dream world. On earth we accept a huge amount of limiting belies. Our bodies are designed and operating within these limiting beliefs controlled by the computer brain.

That is why we suffer physically as we start to remember this is only a dream and start clearing those limiting beliefs. We are told this is our DNA changing, but since the DNA doesn't exist anymore than the body, what really changes are the beliefs we are holding on to. Your DNA is your beliefs.

We have chosen to experience this in the form of physical discomfort to see if that will stop us from remembering and remain within the limiting beliefs of this dream. When you let go of enough beliefs you will realize the physical pain existed only because of your beliefs.

Our goal here is to remember that everything we are told that exists, is only a dream and that the only thing limiting what we can do and experience is what we accept as a belief.

Technology is used to change our beliefs but not to get rid of them (still limitations).

Think that 100 years ago if you told someone that one day they could carry a device the size of a deck of cards that allows them to talk with anyone anywhere in the world they would think you were crazy. That's because their belief system didn't see it as possible.

As the telegraph was developed and then phones, computers, and cell phones peoples beliefs of what was possible changed by what they saw and experienced, but they are still limited because they still believe they need these devices to communicate with someone else.

The idea of a person running a sub 4 minute mile used to be considered impossible.

Then one day a person who didn't accept that as a belief ran a mile under 4 minutes. Within a short time others were able to run sub 4 minute miles. What changed that allowed one person and then others to suddenly do what was thought impossible? The only thing that changed was the belief it was impossible.

Our limiting beliefs are enforced everyday by input from our five senses. We get motion sickness riding a rollercoaster, throw up or get diarrhea from eating food that doesn't agree with us. Get tired and frustrated while sitting in rush hour traffic. We fall, hit ourselves, and trip over things that leave us injured or with pain.

We go to work, maybe get pissed off at our boss or a customer, and watch the sun come up and go down each day. We feel the rain, cold, or heat on our body when outside, and feel the cool softness when lying on the damp grass.

Illness, sickness, and disease seem to strike everyone at some point because we see others having those experiences and its part of our DNA (beliefs). We taste foods and get hungry. Everything we touch enforces the idea that things around us are solid and real.

It is so easy with all the programs of limitation and control running in this dream world to get caught up in believing it is real and that anything beyond this reality isn't real. If you watch the movie, "Inception," it talks about this with a little different twist.

It's because of these overwhelming default beliefs that most people think they can't leave this world (dream) without help.

Many believe so deeply that this world is real they would fight to stay within this dream. The movie the Matrix states this very well.

When we decide to learn about the metaphysical realm or the world of conspiracy theories-facts we are opening ourselves to possibilities that lie outside the traditional brain washing and this allows us to start letting go of those belief systems one step at a time. That is the purpose of healers and energy workers, to help us see possibilities outside of what we have been taught.

Entering the metaphysical realms-beliefs systems also presents problems because they are just additional layers of beliefs we have to move through, but are often times we see them as the end game.

We can start to believe that those new ideas are the final answer and are somehow more real than what we believed before.

We can start accepting that this world isn't real, yet for some reason we will believe the other worlds of supposedly more advanced being are real and if we could just get there we would be real too. As I said before those beings are just us in dreams where they-we have less limiting beliefs to overcome but they are no more real than we are.

I think the people in the earth dream who have a strong feeling they came from another world to help the people of this dream are still having some recall of the world (dream) they were in before they came here.

They are often able to let go of limiting beliefs faster because they haven't been in this dream as long and got caught as deep as most dreamers.

What you might be asking now is how we overcome these limiting beliefs and get out of this dream and have more control over what happens here? I am still working on that process but will share what information I have so far.

The first step is recognizing that we are in a dream and are the creators of that dream and can do anything. Remember you can't get free of a prison that you don't believe you are in.

This first step alone has helped me start getting results the way I wanted. It's the difference between believing you are a slave of the dream, subject to-of the created systems and being a creator of the dream-system in which you have the power to change things.

It's the difference between meeting-talking to the right person that can help you or meeting someone who can't or doesn't want to. The change in flow was pretty obvious to me as it was happening.

These changes were not instantly manifested meaning the things I was dealing with didn't just go away, but when I needed to deal with the issues I got the results I wanted. I didn't focus on how I wanted it to happen just what I wanted it to be and then let it go.

Part of this process that I think is important is becoming more in line with the flow of your life. It's following your inner instinct rather than making decisions in your head. I found that after this experience I was having a hard time planning ahead as I used to do. I was only dealing with what I could at that time and not being concerned with anything beyond that moment.

I was allowing the flow of my dream to guide me knowing I had already set up what was needed to obtain the outcome that was best. Kind of like living in the moment but it was different as well. Focusing on the results not the process which is like the law of attraction but different as well.

By lining up with your inner self-flow you will quickly notice the times when your ego mind wants to direct your path. It wants to own-control the path and the results rather than letting it flow naturally. When you are flowing you will be guided to the people and places you need to be when you need to be there.

Another thing that helped was going in to a meditation state and focus on entering another dream reality with the understanding that within the other dreams you can do anything.

At first you may be unable to do some things in the other dream. Pay attention when this happens because it is showing you some of the beliefs you are holding on to in the earth dream world.

These beliefs carry over to other dreams worlds which I realized is a good thing because you can use that process to change this dream world. It seems to be a 2 way process with one dream having impact on the other dreams in both directions.

What I have been working on is getting conscious control of me in the new dream world. As I do that I am taking things from here that I want to change and creating them-make those changes in the other dream. I do this because in the other dream there are less limiting beliefs which makes it easier to change things.

Once I change what I took from this earth dream and placed in the other dream, I can return to the earth dream and the change here should occur much faster.

I think as I am able to let go of more limiting beliefs on this level I will get access to more dreams with even less limitations and this could make the changes here happen instantly. At that point I would be able travel to any dream world, teleport within the earth dream, and do anything I wanted within this dream.

I am still working on this process and getting more control over me in the dream world.

What it comes down to is this world-reality and all others are just dreams created in order for source/us to experience a thought. I believe this 3D world is about the deepest dream level we can go because of all the default limiting beliefs and controls on us.

Many aspects of source have been in this dream so long they have gotten lost and believe this world and our physical body is real and all that is. They have accepted the default programming so deeply they refused to think about anything beyond this existence.

I think earth was a dream experiment to see how deeply beings could go in to a world of limiting beliefs before they would get lost and believe it was real. We could say the experiment was successful when we look at the people around us, what they believe, and what they are willing to do to others and themselves in order to remain in this dream and accumulate as much power-control, and material reality as they can.

I and many others have come to this dream reality for the first time and we have done so in order to remind people what is real and true. The goal is to start waking people up to the programs they are trapped within so we reclaim all aspect of ourselves and experience other time lines. Question your beliefs and determine if they are really yours or what has been imposed upon you by others. You have the power to change your beliefs, thus your reality, the choice is yours.

CHAPTER 14

Freewill agreements and noninterference by outside forces, truth or another program?

THERE IS A LOT OF agreement among the metaphysical community that there are two laws of the universe that all beings must live by.

First that no being can impose upon or take away the free will of another and the second that there is a policy of noninterference with other worlds and beings.

These are two laws I have to laugh at when I look at all the information that is being written and discussed about the off world beings that are watching and visiting earth to help humanity and others to control humanity. If there was a policy of noninterference why do we have so much information about off world beings?

Many off world-spirit beings are channeled by humans and gladly answer our questions and give us information about our world and theirs. Others are allowing their ships to be seen all over the world.

These same worlds are sending their people to incarnate on earth and make changes from inside by going back in time to effect the decisions humans are making now so as to change their-our future.

Plus they have reportedly changed human DNA many times in the past, and that they have assisted in wiping out past civilizations to create new gene pools. Put all this information together and you will see the idea of noninterference is pure bullshit.

To me the idea of noninterference is like the prime directive on Star Trek where they aren't supposed to even be seen by less advanced civilizations much less change their DNA or come back in time to change their decisions. I'm not sure who came up with the idea that a law of noninterference exists because all the evidence points to the contrary.

The other idea is that we have free will and that they aren't allowed to interfere with our free will and that we have to be asked and agree before they can do anything. It seems to me that anything they would do even if asked would violate the noninterference law.

It is claimed they can get around the free will rule because humans don't say no. On this world and apparently off world, the law agrees that if a person-people don't say no it means they agree to whatever it is. The fact that most people don't know this or have any idea what is being done by off world-spirit beings, doesn't seem to matter. Their running things here seems to be acceptable even if the information about what they are doing is hidden in half truths, outright lies, or in places where people would have to know what they were searching for in order to find the truth.

I know the law in the U.S. agrees that if you don't say no you are saying yes because at one time I was the president of an 1195 home, home owners association. We were starting a law suit against the developer and various builders because of construction defects and various financial agreements they hadn't met.

In order to start this law suit we needed 2/3 of the home owners agree to move forward. When I told the attorney handling the case we can't even get 10% of them to vote in elections or other issues, he said that it doesn't matter. That if they don't send in a no vote, that under the law it is agreed that they must have said yes to whatever the issue was.

Another way they might get around the freewill concept is by creating fear in humans. When you are afraid of something you are afraid of what might happen. It means in your mind you are saying that you expect this to happen and are there for giving it permission to happen. Even though you are saying out loud that you don't want it to happen, by expecting or anticipating it you are saying yes it can happen.

When you look at all the facts about what is going on with off world beings and their dealings with earth, it is pretty obvious there is no law of noninterference or law of free will on any level. It appears that any being from any world is able to come here and do what they want as long as they can get away with it.

CHAPTER 15

Evolution of the human agenda and wave X.

I STARTED THINKING ABOUT WHAT those behind the scenes are doing and what their goal would be in regards to the human population if they got their choice of which time line we would follow.

I think it starts with our parents those born in the1930's and 40's because I think they were the beginning of the current programming cycle. They are a pretty healthy generation which would be needed in order to create a strong base from which to start their next phase of DNA changes within humans.

Most of our parents grew up on home grown and home cooked food, clean water and air. They didn't have all the vaccinations, chem. trails, food full of hormones and antibiotics, credit cards, massive debt, and weren't subject to the electronic vibration influence-controls. They read books and magazines, got together with family and went outside, and listened to the radio for entertainment.

My generation those born in the 1950's and 60's were the first group to really be exposed to television, frozen, processed, prepackaged, and additive loaded food, vaccinations, the expanding of major international corporations, regular jet and airline flights overhead, chem.-trails, medicines, health care programs, widely available drugs and alcohol, and the introduction of the electronic world including computers, cell phones, expanding of mass media, portable music devices with head phones, video games, and let's not forget extensive nuclear testing and fluoride in the water.

Those behind the scene had WW1, WW2, the Korean, and Vietnam Wars to work on their chemical, physical, and psychological programs of DNA change and controlling the human population with plenty of help from off world beings.

They started working to break down the family unit, divide and separate people in to smaller groups by money, politics, clubs, sexes, race, religion, and color, thus making them easier to control and keeping them distracted from what was happening to them.

They wanted both parents and the newly encouraged single parents to be working so there would be less home cooking of real food and more using of prepared additive filled food and using of the new fast food places that were springing up around our country.

Now that they had a strong base to work from (us) they started making changes in our DNA through chemicals as additives in our food, air, water and medical vaccinations.

They began huge programs of behavior control through TV, movies, and in school by telling parents what to feed and do with their children, thus taking more government, actually corporation control over our everyday lives.

Our children those born in the 70's and 80's were the first group to grow up with widely available and considered a part of everyday life electronics including, television with more channels, computers, cell phones, and head phones. They had advances in medical care and medicines, and an increase in vaccinations. They considered being in debt a part of life so had no problems wanting and buying every new electronic device that came out. They started accepting broken families and the separation of people in to groups as normal. This was all part of the program to get them separated from each other, face to face contact, in order to get them interested in using electronic devices to stay in contact.

The DNA changes that had been made in us were being advanced in our children through electronic vibration signals. The additives that had been put in our food, air, water, along with vaccinations and more medicines was been passed on to our children which made them more susceptible and open to the electronic signals they were being flooded and changed with. They continued to ingest the additives in the air, food, and water but weren't as affected by it as we were because it was now a part of their DNA.

Their children, our grandchildren, born over the last 25 years are being born in to a world where microelectronic devices and the desire for them to be more powerful, faster, smaller, and more connected is all that matters.

Watch any kid with a cell phone and you can see where all their attention goes.

The family units that had been broken down have become accepted as normal, people have been separated in to smaller and smaller groups each fighting for special rights and privileges. Having massive debt is considered normal so there is no hesitation to run out and buy the latest electronic device in order to stay instantly but distantly connected.

Phone contracts and programs have become more inclusive, available, and necessary so that even young children have their own phones and computers as soon as they can push a button or talk. Children are encouraged to use these devices in every area of their lives to the point where person to person contact is becoming more limited between them yet the desire to stay in constant contact and more connected is growing.

They desire the human contact but have begun to believe the best way to get it is through an electronic device rather than person to person. Just look at a group of kids hanging out and see what they are all doing, looking at their phones rather than each other and most the time they are texting the person next to them rather than talking.

This generation of children will be the first to readily accept physical electronic implants so they can connect faster and stay connected longer. They will jump at the chance to not have to carry around and lose their phones because it will be a part of their body.

They will no longer worry about the battery running down or losing a signal because their body will be the power source and antenna.

Having these implants will allow those pushing the buttons to have even more control over the DNA changes and they will be able to influence-control the mental and physical attitudes and abilities of these children on every level.

Having these implants as a part of everyday life will make the next step of improved artificial body parts become accepted as normal. The new body parts will allow people to live longer, do more, and even delay aging.

One important thing that is being accomplished by separating this group from personal contact with each other is they are beginning to see other humans not as humans but as another species. This means they are more willing to stand by and watch others being harmed or in trouble because they are losing the human connection.

The next generation of children, our great grand children will be the group to start accepting artificial body parts as normal everyday life and it may even start when they are born to replace parts and organs that aren't prefect and to install the computer connection device for use as they get older. At this point it will give those pushing the buttons complete control over humans and their goal will be reached in only 4 generations.

What is their goal? It's to turn humans in to bio-robots over which they will have complete electronic control.

They can then use humans as slave labor and soldiers in their plans to take over other planets for their resources and additional slave labor.

This might sound crazy to you unless you have done some background research on Enki and his son Marduk who are supposed to be the Anunnaki that are controlling-running this planet as they have for the last 500,000 or so years.

According to the Sumerian text and other writings their goal is to take over the Orion system-empire which is where Enki was born but was kicked out of a long time ago. Humans are going to be his way of gaining entrance to Orin because his mother, the Queen, was the one who created humans and she would welcome them home.

This time line is known as the machine-tech world time line and the one those behind the scenes want us to stay in-on. The good thing is I believe enough of us have come here from our future on the machine-tech time line to have changed our point of awareness from that time line to one where we will take the more spiritual less tech timeline.

This in turn will change the entire universe and all the beings within it. Remember we wouldn't actually change anything except where our awareness is and the time line we would be following.

It may be that the machine-tech time line has played out and been followed to its end and now it's time for us-all beings to shift our awareness to another time line and experience-follow it to the end.

This may be how we experience all the possibilities with our awareness.

If you remember from the chapter on time travel how it works, you will understand that the only way we can have a different future is to move our awareness and not change what happens.

It may be that humans-earth at this point in space time are the key to changing time line awareness since all beings in this universe are humans either past or future.

It may be that as each time line possibility is played out completely-experienced that we have to come back to this point in space time in order to change which time line our awareness will follow from this point forward. This has been feeling right to me and I will have to see where this idea takes me and will write more on it in the future as I get more information.

Wave X

This time line change actually plays in to what is being called wave X. This is supposed to be a wave of energy located at this point in the galaxy and our planet is passing through this wave which was supposed to peak in Sept. 2015.

What I have come to know is that this energy wave is actually us. I say this because wave X is all the universes, realities, and time lines (possibilities) that came off-from this time line-reality we are on-in now from the last 26,000 year cycle.

We have sent aspects-energies of ourselves out along all of those other realities and those aspects-energies of us are now coming back to us because those realities have played out.

There are now enough of us here that have decided the spiritual time line is what we are going to focus on and follow.

All of those other realities-possibilities from the machine world time line are collapsing-dissolving and our energies, the energies we used to create and sustain them, are returning to us so we can become one again and start the process along a different time line. We may send those aspects-energies of us along the new time line to experience all those possibilities.

I guess this answers the question about whether all the other possibilities that created other realties based on our decisions have their own ending or all come back to one time line at some point. They all end up coming back to this time line.

The goal of those behind the scenes, using chem. Trails, CERN, HARP, and all the other energy-vibration programs were to prop up and stop the collapse of those other realities because they wanted us to take-choose another time line in which those running this world could-would continue to exist running this matrix.

They are from what we know as the 4D universe-reality and their hybrid partners on earth that developed-control all the programs of limitation we have been operating under, including all religions and any beings that operate within or are connected to them, ascended masters, charkas, and light bodies, money, government, laws, the tunnel of light, and the list goes on.

The entire 4D reality-universe will only exist as long as we keep-kept the other time line-realities-possibilities sustained.

Once we decided that the spiritual time line-reality was the one we are going to follow (actually we shifted the end of 2011 and early 2012) they knew they didn't have much time left before their reality would start to disappear.

As our energies return to us we will be able to do all the things we have heard we are supposed to be able to do, things like teleporting, moving from one universe-reality to another at will, heal our bodies, telepathy, manifest anything, and so on.

These abilities are a natural part of what we should be able to do as spirit beings. As the 4D beings through their programs of limitation and control caused us to create more realities giving them more energy, we sent more of our energies-aspects to those realities-time lines. This weakened humans to the point where they could only accept this reality as being real.

Those of us that came here from our future did so in order to help each of you to realize you have been programmed since birth to accept this world and all its limitations.

It is only by starting to understand and accept this idea that you will be free enough and able to absorb the aspects of you that came with wave X. This will allow you to change your point of awareness from this controlled reality to one where you will remember who and what you are and have the freedom to leave or explore this universe.

Not understanding and accepting that you are more than human will keep your awareness stuck in this matrix controlled reality on a repeating loop for a long, long time.

FINAL THOUGHTS

I want to thank you for joining me on our journey in a continuing search for the truth. I am honored to be a part of your journey and to have you share mine for however long that will be.

You were probably drawn to and read this book because you were already feeling something is wrong with what you have been taught and the accepted truths-beliefs of this world.

That feeling shows you have made the connection to your subconscious and are in the process of changing your beliefs and your reality, so you will no longer be controlled by the limitations of this world.

I have explained what we are beyond this physical body, how we connect to our higher self, and that in fact our higher self is us, and that there is no one above or beyond us.

You now understand that we are only trapped in this dream reality for as long as we want when we know the truth, and that you don't need a savior to help you leave this system because that power of freedom-salvation belongs to each of us.

You no longer have to be a slave or servant of the system once you reclaim your power as creators, along with the rights and privileges of that position.

We explored some of the controlling programs of this world like sin, karma, fear, reincarnation, time, love, that the words you use does matter, and free will.

If anything you read in this book caused you to see those concepts differently than you did before or made you stop, question, and examine your beliefs, than my intention for writing this book was successful.

I don't expect everyone to agree with everything I wrote because each of us sees and understands things differently, and each of us will have different experiences.

Take what feels right and see where that information-path will lead you. Remember you don't have to follow my path if it doesn't feel right.

This book has different levels of information and each time you read it you will gain-see more information because of what you learned in reading it before. I would suggest that after reading it the first time you set it aside, go about your life, and when you feel the time is right reread it.

Please share with others what you learn on your search for the truth because as I wrote at the beginning of the book, the truth is owned by all.

Now that you have finished this book I want you to understand, I didn't write this book to tell you what to think, I wrote it to get you to think.